LITTLE BROTHER,
MUCH LOVE,
TAJ

Blows Against the Empire...

11/14/08

Gerald Horne

BLOWS
AGAINST THE
EMPIRE

U.S. IMPERIALISM IN CRISIS

GERALD HORNE

INTERNATIONAL PUBLISHERS, *New York*

1st edition 2008
International Publishers Co., Inc.
All Rights Reserved

LCCN 2008922076

ISBN 978-0-7178-0746-8

Table of Contents

Blows Against the Empire...

Introduction: The Crisis of U.S. Imperialism

The entire island of Puerto Rico was riveted.

As palm trees swayed and ocean waves crashed lazily on the shore of this Caribbean colony, jaws dropped and eyes glistened with tears as they strained to watch the image on their television sets when the mother of slain Army Corporal Jason Núñez, a mere 22 years of age, angrily removed the alien U.S. flag draping his coffin and deliberately dropped it to the floor. Later she implored other parents not to allow their children to fight for the U.S. military—least of all in the conflict in Iraq that had claimed her child's life.

This stirring scene from March 2007 pithily illustrated why the criminal and illegal U.S. invasion of Iraq and the attempt to impose a brutal colonial rule on this proud nation and people is now routinely described—even by those who stroll the corridors of power—as the most serious foreign policy disaster in recent U.S. history. For not only is Washington spending billions of taxpayer dollars in a failed attempt to dominate Iraq and the region, just as it imposed its diktat on tiny Puerto Rico more than a century ago, this is occurring as a tectonic shift is taking place globally, as China continues its inexorable peaceful rise.

Despite the diabolical and demonic schemes of the present occupant of the White House, the insistent cry of Jason Nunez's mother is being heeded. For just as the great scholar-activist W.E.B. Du Bois pointed to what amounted to a "general strike" among enslaved Africans was the final nail in the coffin of the devilish dream of the Southern states of the U.S. to overthrow the government in order to perpetuate human bondage, today those who have been designated as cannon fodder for the war machine are refusing to fight and, thereby, are contributing mightily to the current and irreversible crisis of U.S. imperialism.

Thus, a staggering 57% of Puerto Rico's 10th, 11th and 12th graders, or their parents, have signed forms over the past year withholding contact information from the Pentagon—effectively barring U.S. recruiters from reaching out to an estimated 65,000 high school students.[1]

Not to be outdone, those who have pioneered in this potent strategy of aversion to joining the legions of death, have been in the vanguard once more. For years, African-Americans have made up nearly 25 percent of the Army, more than twice their representation in the general population but by February 2005, this number had dropped to 13.9%. This stems directly from a blazing anti-war sentiment spreading like wildfire in this traditionally progressive constituency. Thus, in April 2003 when the war in Iraq seemed to be the cakewalk it had been bruited to be, a Gallup Poll revealed that 78% of whites yet only 29% of Blacks supported the war.[2]

Increasingly, the militantly antiwar sentiments of Puerto Ricans and African-Americans are spreading beyond these two communities, presenting yet another obstacle strewn in the path of U.S. imperialism.

Rebekah Roberts, a 24 year old mother of a two year old residing in Scranton, Pennsylvania, might be able to explain why. As Corporal Núñez was being mowed down in the sands of Iraq, this member of the military reserves found herself stationed in this same country. She was worried about the enemy—but not the one the White House had in mind. Yes, she was worried about snipers, ambushes, and improvised explosive devices—but she had a further dire concern: her fellow soldiers. From 2002 to 2006 more than 500 women soldiers serving in Iraq or Afghanistan have been sexually assaulted, leading these troops to devise crafty methods to avoid being attacked by their "comrades," just as their male counterparts have sought to being assaulted by Iraqis and Afghanis.[3]

*   *   *

Certainly, the murderous attack on civilians on 11 September 2001 provided the Bush regime with an opportunity to unleash its already percolating war plans. But Z. Pallo Jordan—a key leader of South Africa's ruling African National Congress—was not alone in pointing to the ineradicable fact that those who had attacked Manhattan on that fateful day had shared the same trench with Washington during the bloody intervention in Afghanistan in the 1980s against the Moscow-backed regime. "The so-called mujahadeen, led by Osama Bin Laden," he argued within days of the assault on New York, had been "an ally of the United States intelligence community for well nigh two decades." His passion growing in intensity, Comrade Jordan asserted vigorously that "the 'bleeding ulcer' of Afghanistan was among the many factors that sapped the strength of the Soviet Union, leading to its collapse."[4]

Of course, there are few among the chattering classes of the U.S. who are as bold in announcing the simple reality that it was precisely the anti-Sovietism of the Cold War that not only empowered a murderous so-called "Islamic fundamentalism" but as well opened the door for massive foreign investment (notably after Richard Nixon's Beijing journey some 35-odd years ago) that has placed China on track to dislodge the U.S. as this planet's most formidable economic force and, likewise, destabilized the domestic left as it propelled forward the draining designs of the right. The problem for U.S. imperialism now is that it is in relative decline in relation to the rising giant that is China, and the European Union particularly, as its remaining advantage—military power—slowly sinks into the sands of Iraq and threatens to erode further if the conservative hawks have their way and Iran is attacked. Moreover, there is a real question—rarely debated—if the influential U.S. right wing are even capable of fighting the rudimentarily right-wing force that is so-called "Islamic fundamentalism." Ineluctably—as if by an "invisible hand"—U.S. conservatism will strengthen so-called Islamic conservatives.

Indirectly, Comrade Jordan's insight has been confirmed by the former National Security Advisor to President Jimmy Carter, Zbigniew Brzezinski. It was under his direction that the U.S. launched the largest "covert" operation in the history of the infamous Central Intelligence Agency. Strangely, future historians will look long and hard for evidence of opposition in the U.S. to this disastrous policy—beyond the confines of those in the orbit of the Communist Party, USA[5]—which resulted in 9/11. With such nonfeasance, Brezinski did not hesitate to boast in early 1998 that "American intelligence services began to aid the Mujahadeen in Afghanistan 6 months before the Soviet intervention"—though all too many in the U.S. continue to subscribe to the fairy tale that Moscow's intervention had nothing to do with the harassment of Kabul by Washington.[6] In a nutshell, the current crisis of U.S. imperialism cannot be divorced from the doctrine of anticommunism.

Unfortunately, like a patient who does not seem to realize that the cream being used to reduce blemishes is actually worsening the problem, Washington cannot seem to avoid collaborating with those with whom it collaborated during the Cold War—with similarly disastrous results awaiting. In a sadly neglected report by ABC News on 3 April 2007, it was noted that Washington is aiding "Jundullah," a group of Baluchis, a minority grouping in Iran, "responsible for a series of deadly guerrilla raids," not to mention "the deaths and kidnappings of more than a dozen Iranian soldiers and officials." According to a commentator on ABC News, this band's leader is "part drug smuggler" and "part Taliban"—i.e. Washington is aiding in Iran those who they are fighting in neighboring Afghanistan.[7]

While wildly beating the drums of war, targeting Afghanistan, then Iraq, now Iran, the venal Bush regime has been busily and greedily dipping their paws in public coffers. Naturally, being an advocate of "family values," Bush has not neglected his "Uncle Bucky"—William Bush—who holds a coveted seat on the board of Engineered Support Systems

Incorporated (ESSI), a St. Louis based company that has flourished mightily as a military contractor to the Pentagon. ESSI has received the prized "no-bid contracts" that have so enriched Halliburton, formerly led by Vice-President Dick Cheney. In January 2005, as ESSI shares reached a record $60.39 apiece, "Uncle Bucky" cashed out, selling a whopping 8,438 options worth around $450,000. Of course, ESSI's fortunes have risen as the quagmire in Iraq has deepened, as this Midwestern giant has supplied $49 million in military trailers and $18 million in "communications services" to Baghdad.[8]

Being a dedicated and conscious class warrior, Bush has not just assisted "Uncle Bucky" but those of his class as well. In early 2002, as the nation was still reeling from 9/11, Bush announced a multi-billion military buildup that brought smiles to the jowly faces of shareholders of Lockheed Martin, Boeing, Raytheon, Northrop Grumman, General Dynamics, Litton, General Electric, United Technologies, TRW and Textron. This occurred as the United Way described Los Angeles County as being in "the most precarious [condition] since the Great Depression." Three million there are deemed to be "poor" and 1.4 million are classified as "food insecure," including 45% of children in poor families.[9]

Yet as millions writhe in the agony of poverty and disease, in August 2007 it was announced that the war in Iraq alone could ultimately cost well over a trillion dollars—or more than 10% of all the government's annually appropriated funds.[10] This occurred as the White House called for slashing an eye-popping $78.6 billion from Medicare and Medicaid over the next five years.[11]

Imperialism bends toward irrationality in any case, yet even this well-worn truism hardly explains the nature of conservatism today. For as challenges to U.S. imperialism mount in Beijing, Havana, Brussels, Moscow, Teheran, Caracas, Brasilia and elsewhere and as the nation cries out for more spending on education and health care, conservatism instead continues to spend almost drunkenly on the military. What has to be grasped is that as a frontline state during the Cold War, the U.S. bent further toward conservatism—notably hostility to the public sector and government itself—than its allies. (Inevitably, this has meant a retreat in democracy, since the public sector can be reached by voters who elects its stewards more readily than the private sector, where one must be a major stockholder to wield such influence.) But now the planet has moved on. State-owned oil companies are challenging private ones like Exxon-Mobil; government subsidized universal health care provides Japanese automakers a distinct advantage over the U.S., where conservatism blocks the adoption of such a rational measure: in sum, conservatism—along with seeking to exclude the left from the political table—is deepening

U.S. imperialism's crisis.

In fact, the rapidly declining dollar inexorably will mean an increase in oil prices for this commodity that is priced in U.S. currency; U.S. voters must consider whether the oil men who now rule this nation—and are quite close to the feudal Saudis who wield influence in oil markets—actually are not terribly upset about the continuing rise in oil prices.

For the fact is that although U.S. imperialism routinely describes itself as the "indispensable nation" and the "sole remaining superpower," it finds itself enmeshed in an irrevocable and irreversible decline that belies the pretensions of its acolytes. Strikingly, this is a consensus that encompasses a broad swath of the ideological spectrum. Niall Ferguson, a Scot who teaches at Harvard while being affiliated with the nursing home of the mind that is the neo-conservative Hoover Institute at Stanford University, has proclaimed that "what befell Venice 500 years ago may well be the imminent fate of its North American counterpart: New York;" i.e. just as this city-state was eclipsed by the rise of Great Britain and Spain, he suggests that China may very well surpass the U.S.[12] From the other shore, the progressive South Asian-born writer, Dilip Hiro, has written contemptuously of "America on the downward slope" and "the rise of a multi-polar world." [13] The Italian writer, Francesco Sisci, also has invoked Venice, noting that William Shakespeare set some of his best plays there—"The Merchant of Venice," and "Othello," for example—in what had been thought to be the most advanced region in the world, though as it turned out the famed playwright was ensconced in what was already the most advanced nation: Britain. And now, he argues, "China's growth has brought a systemic change to the world at large," which "foreshadows a different world, where for the first time in at least two centuries the West [sic] will become an economic minority." [14]

Thus, while the right-wing bathes unworriedly in the muck of national chauvinism, the nation over which they preside is undergoing a profound crisis. Marxists have spoken confidently of the "general crisis of capitalism," said to have been ignited by the October Revolution of 1917, then propelled by the rise of a socialist camp, the existence of a sturdy working class movement, not least in the metropole, and national liberation movements in what had been the colonized world. The fall of the Berlin Wall in 1989 and the collapse of the Soviet Union in 1991 was thought by some to have eviscerated capitalism's general crisis.

Setting that debate aside, there is little doubt that those who felt that these epochal events had turbo-charged U.S. imperialism have been sadly mistaken. The evidence abounds. In fact, just as the rise of so-called "Islamic fundamentalism" is tied inextricably to the anti-Sovietism that animated the U.S. intervention in Afghanistan in the 1980s, this Moscow-centric doctrine also propelled Washington to back the concept of European unity—which eventuated in today's 500 million strong European Union—that is now bedeviling the declining fortunes of U.S. imperialism.

For example, the euro—the currency of Washington's ally cum competitor, the European Union—has replaced the dollar as the world's pre-eminent currency in the all-important international bond market. Dumbfounded, the *Financial Times* of London announced quizzically, that this "represents a startling turnabout from the pattern seen in recent decades, when the U.S. bond market dwarfed its European rival: as recently as 2002," Wall Street was in the lead—but not anymore.[15] This is a handmaiden to the fact that increasingly nations are abandoning the dollar in favor of the euro—indeed, the allegation has been made that Saddam Hussein's decision to do so was a factor in his overthrow. It was in February 2006 that Iraq's neighbor, Syria, announced that it was dropping the dollar in favor of the euro.[16] This is no small matter, not only because to that point Damascus held billions in dollars but also because this amounted to an interest free loan to a cash-strapped Washington. A stampede away from the dollar would be of profound significance financially.

Similarly, in years gone by the seal of approval for, say, a Korean steel manufacturer, would be having its accounts conform to the U.S. based accounting principles, known as GAAP. But today the non-U.S., IFRS standard is the global norm. As one business columnist put it, "and so the reins of power slip further from American fingers." Jubilant capitalists in London chortled that "it now seems a given that they inhabit the financial capital of the world. New York is regarded almost with condescension."[17]

It was in the Spring of 2007 that Robert Pozen, a member in good standing of the U.S. ruling elite, announced morosely that "in the past six months, three studies have been published on the declining role of the U.S. in global capital markets......of the 10 largest global IPOs [initial public offerings of stock shares] in 2005, eight were headquartered in China and Europe, so they launched in the Hong Kong and European markets." This trend, combined with others, he predicted sadly, "will prevent the U.S. from regaining the dominant position of the mid-1990s."[18] The export of capital has been the hallmark of U.S. imperialism and helped to propel it into the front rank of imperialist nations—but the times are changing.

The industrial decline of U.S. imperialism is well-known. Once it was said that "what is good for General Motors is good for the nation" as this industrial behemoth was seen—by some—as the bell-cow of imperialism. But it was only recently that GM, Ford and Chrysler "suffered the humiliation"—as the *Financial Times* waspishly put it—"of seeing their home market share sink below 50 percent for the first time."[19]

Even Hollywood, where global domination had been thought to be a God-given right, has been in retreat. In the Spring of 2007, 7 of the top 10 movies at the South Korean box office were made in Seoul, China or Japan. French films accounted for 46% of the total box office in France in 2006, up from 35% in 2005. As the *Los Angeles Times* put it, "anti-Americanism"—i.e. hostility to U.S. imperialism—is hampering the profiteering of the movie studios.[20]

This relative decline of U.S. imperialism has emboldened its rivals, all of whom have more sizeable progressive movements and correspondingly, less potent conservatives. Because U.S. imperialism was at the tip of the spear during the Cold War conflict with the former Soviet Union, it felt compelled to accentuate almost hysterically the ideology of deregulation and privatization and bowing down obediently before the diktat of capital. This has meant that executives here are compensated much more handsomely than their counterparts abroad. But in a move destined to be duplicated in other spheres, the union activists who have been clamoring and complaining about this unjust enrichment have now been joined by allies abroad. The U.S. rule giving shareholders no say on executive compensation contrasts with the system in Australia, the Netherlands, Sweden and the U.K. Now overseas investors are insisting that their global rules be adopted by U.S. corporations, which has added wind to the sails of similar demands of union-backed pension funds.[21] Fewer millions—and billions—going to these captains of industry can be the difference in determining whether U.S. workers will enjoy retirement—or scrounge for dog food.

The point is that the U.S. working class and mass movement either must take advantage of what has been termed (euphemistically) as globalization by forging tighter bonds abroad—or fall victim to our antagonists who are determined to turn global forces against us.

Likewise, August 2007 witnessed the onset of a global financial meltdown ignited by a deregulated mortgage industry that was the essence of the "cowboy capitalism" that has been de rigueur on these shores. Instead of the government guaranteeing affordable housing and/or providing adequate compensation in wages, in the U.S. the working class is loaded down with credit and debt and instructed to wander into the vagaries of the "free market" to gain shelter. In short, U.S. manipulators sliced and diced dodgy mortgage loans and sold them—particularly abroad—while investors relied on the word of "rating agencies" like Moody's and Standard & Poor's that all was well as these loans were bundled into bonds and peddled like snake oil. The problem was that all was not well as Wall Street unleashed the equivalent of a nasty computer virus that led to the collapse of at least one German bank, while the Bank of China suffered billions in losses. In response the European Union—whose regulations already have become a global standard in various realms in a direct affront to the U.S. mantra of deregulation—announced portentously that it would be investigating these agencies, which no doubt will lead to an alteration in how capitalism is practiced on these shores.[22]

A seemingly flabbergasted *New York Times* reporter, announced with apparent astonishment that "politicians, regulators and financial specialists outside the United States are seeking a role in the oversight of American markets, banks and rating agencies after recent problems related to subprime mortgages." Professor Dick Bryan of the University of Sydney in Australia stated what was evident when he asserted, "there is the need to challenge the sovereignty" of the U.S., as the "consequences" of actions here "go everywhere." [23] Similarly, the "consequences" of what occurs abroad has impact here—which is why leading U.S. economists have concluded that trends beyond these shores increasingly are handcuffing the ability of the powerful Federal Reserve Bank in Washington to reduce inflation—or deflation—here.[24] Of late, *The New York Times* worried nervously about the impact in this nation of so-called "Sovereign Wealth Funds" (vehicles established by states, e.g. Singapore, Norway, etc. to seek a higher return on their growing foreign exchange holdings): These funds may control "a staggering $17. 5 trillion dollars in 10 years." "What would the reaction be," the newspaper of record wondered nervously, "if an Arab government demanded a bailout or tax break for its company in return for supporting peace talks in Iraq or Israel?" [25] The impending tidal wave of foreign investment into the U.S., driven by those abroad unwilling to continue accepting devalued dollars, will cause many to call into question the presently dominant rhetoric of "free markets"—which will further expose the hypocrisy of U.S. imperialism.

This "challenge" to U.S. sovereignty opens up new vistas for progressive forces in this nation. For example, it is now acknowledged that what helped to propel the agonized retreat of U.S. imperialism from the most atrocious aspects of Jim Crow was global pressure: Washington found it difficult to posture as a paragon of human rights virtue in the battle of ideas with the socialist camp when it treated such a huge percentage of its citizenry so horribly.[26] The strategic question for the mass movement and the working class in the U.S. today is how to leverage this proliferating global influence for progressive gain at home—and abroad.

For the combination of the relative decline of U.S. imperialism, along with its continuing noxious impact, has invigorated even other imperialists. Jacques Chirac of France was notorious in 2003 for his staunch opposition to the U.S. invasion of Iraq, a position hailed and played upon by antiwar forces on these shores. Garnering less publicity was his demand in early 2007 that Washington sign both the Kyoto climate protocol and a future agreement that will take effect when the Kyoto accord expires in 2012. He warned that if this reasonable step did not occur, the U.S. would face a carbon tax across Europe—still this nation's most important market—in order to compel compliance.[27] Similarly, it has been the E.U. that has been in the forefront of demanding that the U.S. drop the barbarous death penalty, which has disproportionately claimed the lives of African-Americans. Brussels' reasonable demand was brought to the doorstep of conservative Texas Governor Rick "The Hairdo" Perry, as Bush's home state approached the dubious though deadly distinction of executing its 400th inmate since 1982.[28] The right-wing chief executive at first derided this demand—before meekly complying and commuting the death sentence of African-American inmate, Kenneth Foster. Similarly, it will be the European Union that reins in the Microsoft monopoly, not the U.S. Justice Department.

Ironically, conservatives—who purport to be the most dedicated patriots—have pursued policies that actually have reduced the range of the nation's sovereignty. This is nothing new: historically the ideological ancestors of today's conservatives backed avidly the Articles of Confederation, which would have weakened the new nation, as against the Constitution subsequently adopted. Then these same forces sought to overthrow the U.S. government when their right to extend slavery was blunted. Now they are incrementally overthrowing that same government—as they wrap themselves in the flag.

Brussels' pressure on Texas was of a piece with its collaboration with California. For it was in March 2007 that a delegation of officials from Sacramento arrived in the EU's capital in order to explore whether the Golden State could join one of Europe's most controversial and ambitious projects: the emissions trading scheme designed to reduce climate change. In sum, California was circumventing Washington and cutting a deal with Brussels—which is not as unusual as it sounds. For as U.S. imperialism remains ensnarled in crisis—and continues to preach a discredited sermon hailing deregulation—the European Union has grown in importance correspondingly to the point where not only states in the U.S. but nations globally are now following Brussels' lead in such disparate areas as product safety, financial regulation, anti-trust, transport, telecommunications, and myriad other policy areas. As was noted in the *Financial Times*, "The EU is increasingly replacing the United States as the de facto setter of global product standards and the centre of much global regulatory setting is shifting from Washington, D.C. to Brussels."[29]

This crisis of U.S. imperialism is also eroding this nation's domination of science, a trend that proved to be decisive during the Cold War. Yet since 2004 when the White House, seeking to compensate for massive tax cuts for the wealthy, called for a reduction in spending, the budget for the National Institutes for Health has been flat and has declined in real terms. As a result, numerous U.S. scientists are fleeing to greener pastures abroad. Bart Anderson of Vanderbilt moved to Australia. Patrick Cavenaugh left Harvard in favor of the University of Paris. "The situation is incredibly bleak," acknowledged Xandra Breakefield of Harvard Medical School. It is not only reduced budgets; some scientists are fleeing because of the stifling of thought and creativity—e.g. in the cutting edge field of stem-cell research, a retreat induced by religious conservatives who rest at the heart of contemporary conservatism.[30] Scientists' fears were not assuaged when the news leaked that Bush claimed a divine mandate to wage war in Afghanistan and Iraq.[31] Moreover, migrants from China and India have fueled technological innovation on these shores— but now a "reverse brain drain" is occurring, as they repatriate to their homelands with gargantuan consequence for the fate of U.S. imperialism.[32]

Thus, the crisis of U.S. imperialism continues unabated. Yet an essential component of this crisis is the continuing hold on power by Communist parties, not least in Beijing and Havana. Though one would not know it from sifting through the propaganda about the "death of communism," the fact is that Marxists were ousted from power in Europe— but not in Latin America or Asia—hardly insignificant on a planet where white supremacy has been a defining trait. And in some ways the key to the collapse in Eastern Europe was the post-1972 imperialist concessions to China, which in some ways meant that Washington simply exchanged a contradiction-plagued relationship with Moscow for a contradiction-plagued relationship with Beijing.

Certainly, China has been essential to the continuing vitality of socialist Cuba, as the commuters traveling on Chinese-made buses or using Chinese-made refrigerators or watching Chinese-made televisions or riding Chinese-made bicycles or utilizing Chinese-made computers could well attest.[33]

Of course, the experience of Cuba is not *sui generis*, as China has become the factory floor for the planet, the manufacturing engine of the global economy with consequences so immense they have yet to be fully grasped. Even in the U.S., the use of Chinese goods has become veritably ubiquitous, as one family recently made news when they sought to live without any goods carrying the label "Made in China."[34]

"The rise of China is now so rapid," said the business columnist

Gideon Rachman, "that Goldman Sachs recently revised its projection for the moment at which the Chinese economy will be larger than that of the U.S. The bank now thinks that China will overtake the U.S. by 2027 (in real dollar terms), rather than by 2035 as previously predicted......India is also catching up fast," he added, and "by 2050 the Indian economy will also be larger than that of the U.S."[35]

The irrationality of the response to this stark challenge to rapidly dissipating U.S. hegemony has struck some as comical, worthy of a monologue by Jay Leno or David Letterman. The "analogy that comes to mind," said the Swiss academic, Jean-Pierre Lehmann, in referring to U.S. proposals for Chinese currency revaluation in order to curb the massive trade deficit with Beijing, "is that of an alcoholic on a binge blaming his drinks supplier for his addiction. Rather than cutting his own consumption substantially, he is demanding that the supplier increase the price of the booze," i.e. "appreciate" the Chinese currency.[36]

The increasing hysteria—and ridiculousness—of Washington's threats targeting China has led to the inevitable: an observer at the fabled Canton Fair in China in April 2007 noticed that "the American market is not as crucial as it used to be" for Beijing, which now avers that their fastest growth nowadays is in Europe, Africa, the Middle East and South America. As China retreats from its dependence on exports to the U.S., this makes Washington's threats even more hollow.[37]

U.S. imperialism's laughable approach to China, in any case, has caused even erstwhile unshakeable allies of U.S. imperialism to find that they have to make adjustments in this "new world order" that George H.W. Bush did not fully comprehend when he enunciated this concept in the immediate wake of the tumultuous regime changes in Eastern Europe. Even Israel, whose fealty to U.S. imperialism has been pronounced, raised eyebrows—and tempers—in Washington as it sought to solidify relations with Beijing when it sought to sell airborne warning and control equipment to China. Before that, Washington was stunned when it recognized Israeli gun turret technology in photographs of tanks used at Tiananmen Square against protesters in the pivotal year of 1989.[38]

As U.S. conservatives have pursued their maniacal policies of shrinking the public sector in pursuit of the Reaganesque notion that "government is the problem," taxpayers have resisted a concomitant reduction in services provided by the government. The shortfall has been made up by central bankers in China who have loaded up on U.S. Treasury bills, thus saving Washington from even more dramatic slashing of education and health care. The realistic Stephen C. Roach, Morgan Stanley's chief economist, writing—strikingly—in *China Daily*—dared to utter an unavoidable reality under conservative rule: "America no longer has the internal wherewithal to fund the rapid growth of its economy," and "is increasingly dependent on surplus foreign savings to fill the void." [39]

Surely, this dependence on Beijing has been chastening for those in Washington still harboring dreams of regime change in China. Gaining less notice is how this state of affairs has engendered increased bravado and confidence in Beijing.

As the global financial meltdown gained traction in August 2007, congressional threats to impose punitive tariffs on Chinese goods mounted. He Fan, an official at the Chinese Academy of Social Sciences, warned that Beijing might liquidate its vast holdings of U.S. dollars—a mind-boggling $1.33 trillion at last count—which was described as China's "nuclear option." This draconian measure would hammer the already tottering U.S. housing market and could tip the economy into a painful recession—or worse.[40] This was not the first time that Beijing threatened to inflict a brutal blow against U.S. imperialism. Days before the Washington visit of President Hu Jintao in the spring of 2006, Cheng Siwei—Vice Chair of the Chinese Parliament—set the tone for this gathering by threatening that Beijing would trim its holdings of U.S. debt and stop buying dollar bonds. According to *Reuters*, this caused "rattling" in financial markets[41] and, no doubt, unease in the Oval Office.

China also has been a driving force behind the formation of the Shanghai Cooperation Organization—which also includes Russia—and, in some ways, is a 21st Century version of the old Warsaw Pact, suggesting once more how the successful crusade against the former Soviet Union may have bought time for U.S. imperialism but did not end its crisis. At their August 2007 meeting, frazzled nerves gripped Washington and Wall Street as the stock market went south; the leaders of China, Russia and— intriguingly—Iran, warned Washington at the annual SCO confab to cease its interference in the internal affairs of Central Asia. This occurred as President Vladimir Putin of Russia and President Hu Jintao of China arrived in the Ural Mountains to observe thousands of heavily armed Russian and Chinese troops, dozens of aircraft and hundreds of armored vehicles participate in well-planned military maneuvers—a pointed message to Washington as to what could ensue if U.S. imperialism continued to pursue its reckless policies.[42]

Increasingly hysterical about perceived challenges to its military hegemony, U.S. imperialism has begun exploring the idea of using outer space for aggressive purposes. The Cuban press, which has good reason to keep a close eye on such hysteria, was struck by the Pentagon's plan to develop a "gay bomb," i.e. a weapon that allegedly would "turn enemy soldiers into homosexuals," supposedly disrupting unit cohesion.[43]

Bigotry has been a hallmark of this settler state—unsurprising in a nation whose founding principles included white supremacy; thus, putrid racism has arisen in the U.S. in the face of China's challenge. Recall the mass internment of Japanese-Americans—and the acquiescence to it by all too many progressive forces—in the midst of the Pacific War, suggesting the abject difficulty that this nation has had in grappling with powerful nations not of European descent. Recall more recently, the Spring of 2001, when Beijing downed a U.S. spy plane on Chinese soil and tensions were ratcheted up by a White House bent on exacting revenge against a nation deemed to be a "strategic competitor." Simultaneously, a tidal wave of noxious racism was unleashed against Chinese-Americans. Taken aback, the *San Francisco Chronicle,* headquartered in a region "where Asian Americans are about 20 percent of the population and where people pride themselves on tolerance," was shocked at the proliferation of "radio high jinks and satiric skits that feature Chinese characters with thick glasses, buck teeth and heavy Asian accents;" some radio commentators called for "Chinese American internment." [44] Similarly, Israel—which really should know better but is having evident difficulty in finding sure footing on a shifting global landscape—had to replace its Ambassador in Australia in 2006 after he proclaimed that his nation and the "lucky country" where he was posted are "white sisters amid 'the yellow race' of Asia." [45]

Rather than engaging in a sober analysis that would indicate that Washington made a strategic blunder when it forged an anti-Soviet alliance that put China into boost phase—not unlike Paris' effort to flummox London by backing the victorious rebels in late 18th century North America—instead U.S. imperialism is seeking a military fix. Their malevolent plans were exposed when the prestigious journal, *Foreign Affairs,* carried a transfixing article in the Spring of 2006 suggesting that Washington has developed nuclear capacity to launch a strike guaranteed to wipe out Russia and China without the risk of suffering a return strike. This was the thinly veiled secret behind the White House's eagerness to install an anti-missile defense system in Eastern Europe—supposedly to foil Iran but actually to blunt a retaliatory strike from Moscow or Beijing. Former Russian Prime Minister Yegor Gaidar grossly understated the point when he concluded that this bug-brained scheme would "provoke Russia and China into close cooperation over missile and nuclear technologies." [46]

This startling dust-up had the advantage, ironically, of clarifying the nature of the decades-long conflict with Moscow. It was not about Stalin's violation of human rights, for how would that account for Nixon toasting Mao? It was about opening of markets with China and being more enthusiastic about this than with the former USSR. It was also about geo-politics in that global domination mandates control of the defining characteristic of this small planet—the land bridge that connects the most populous continent, Asia, with the richest: Europe. And that requires subordination or acquiescence of the two key nodes—China and Russia. Yet now U.S. imperialism finds itself in the unenviable position of deteriorating relations with both.

For although Moscow has proved itself to be capital-friendly, it has hardly become acquiescent to U.S. imperialism, notably since the dislodging of the disastrous reign of Boris Yeltsin. Most recently, President Putin demanded a downgrading of both the International Monetary Fund and the World Bank—the twin towers of imperialist domination. He said that more than 60% of the world's output was produced outside the heretofore hegemonic nations, i.e. the U.S., UK, France, Germany, Italy, Canada and Japan, and therefore global institutions should reflect this new order.[47]

Inevitably, Washington hawks have sought to cloak their hypocritical opposition to Beijing's peaceful development in the appealing garments of human rights. Yet this gambit has opened the door to China raising searching questions about the state of human rights in the U.S., which—again—opens new vistas for advance on this all-important front. Their primary focus was on police brutality in the U.S. itself and the atrocities committed in Iraq by U.S. troops. Tellingly, Beijing bemoaned the fact that "racial discrimination has been deeply rooted in the United States, permeating into every aspect of society.....the proportion for persons of colored races [sic] being sentenced or being imprisoned is notably higher than whites."[48]

The crisis of U.S. imperialism has encouraged nations besides China to scrutinize more critically the unfortunate internal situation in this country. The main human rights watchdog of the United Nations has rebuked Washington because of its deficient asylum and immigration rules, its frequent use of the death penalty, the imposition of life sentences on children, festering police brutality and ill-treatment in prisons.[49] In a welcome development, Jorge A. Bustamante, the special rapporteur on human rights of the U.N., spent two days in Los Angeles in the Spring of 2007 taking voluminous testimony about worker abuse and related issues. In particular he took note of the brutal police attack on peaceful pro-immigrant demonstrators that had occurred on May Day.[50] This scrutiny reached a crescendo in the aftermath of Hurricane Katrina in 2005, which exposed the ugly sore of U.S. racism. Comments from the global press were voluminous and were aggregated by *Granma* of Cuba. Typical were the remarks in the *Daily Nation* of Kenya, which was struck by "the images, and even the disproportionately high number of visibly impoverished blacks among the [displaced] could easily have been a re-enactment of a scene from the pigeonholed African continent."

Le Temps of Switzerland observed that the "sea walls would not have burst in New Orleans if the funds meant for strengthening them had not been cut to help the war effort in Iraq and the war on terror….and rescue work would have been more effective if a section of the National Guard from the areas affected had not been sent to Baghdad and Kabul." Yet intriguingly it was added that "would George Bush have left his holiday ranch more quickly if the disaster had not first struck the most disadvantaged populations of the black south?" [51]

In a remarkable parallel, the statement from the premier U.S. based anti-war grouping, United for Peace and Justice, mirrored comments emerging from Switzerland and Kenya, indicating the gathering domestic and global sentiment mounting against the malfeasance of U.S. conservatives, suggesting the incipient formation of today's strategic imperative: an all-peoples' global front against U.S. imperialism: "In both the Persian and American gulfs," it was noted, "the poorest people suffer most…..why are 35-40% of the Louisiana and Mississippi National Guards in Iraq, on missions of death, instead of back home where they are so desperately needed?" [52]

The recognition that imperialism is the central question—as evidenced by the hegemonic antiwar sentiments among Puerto Ricans and African-Americans—is growing. Local 600 of the United Auto Workers, which represents 30,000 active and retired members in Michigan has been in the forefront of opposition to the war in Iraq.[53] They are far from being alone. Before the onset of this disastrous conflict, U.S. Labor Against the War was in the vanguard of an effort that culminated in 200 unions and 550 union leaders from 53 countries representing 130 million workers signing the International Labor Declaration opposing imperialist aggression. "This is the first time in history," it was asserted, "that the world's labor movements have come together to speak with a single voice on an issue of urgent international concern." At the same time, these global unions were conspicuous in their presence in the marches of millions that occurred globally in order to stay the hand of the U.S. invasion.[54] The AFL-CIO, which includes a number of unions that backed the war against Vietnam, early on declared its opposition to the catastrophic war against Iraq.[55] By the summer of 2007 a total of 300 towns, cities and states—encompassing about 50% of the U.S.'s population of 300 million—had passed resolutions opposing the occupation of Iraq.[56]

It is well that there has been a confluence of domestic and global opposition to U.S. imperialism, for the tactics used on one front by Washington are rapidly being transferred to the other. That was the import of a judge's decision in Chicago in May 2006 that a special prosecutor's report on accusations of torture by police there should be made public, as a UN panel in Geneva urged U.S. authorities to investigate the claims further. The investigation stemmed from accusations by 192 persons that Chicago police officers tortured them with electric devices. These charges were made as the question of torture at Abu Ghraib prison in Iraq, and the U.S. detention center at Guantanamo Bay, were gathering steam. Close observers recognized that torture abroad inevitably generated torture at home—and vice versa: both reflected imperialism in crisis.[57]

There is a growing acknowledgement that the relative decline of U.S. imperialism, combined with advances in the means of communication—including the Internet, sophisticated supply chains, supersonic transport and the like—are reworking the meaning of labor in this nation. According to Princeton economist Alan Blinder, tens of millions of jobs in the U.S. are subject to being "offshored" or "outsourced" in coming years. And even if these 56 million jobs do not depart for Bangalore or Burundi, workers in Baltimore will still be in direct competition with these workers overseas. These are not only factory workers—the usual suspects—but also architects and tax lawyers and computer programmers. This is a problem that merely upgrading skills and more education cannot solve, in other words.

The remedy must lie in global solidarity of the international working class, particularly against the primary threat to international peace and security—U.S. imperialism. Globalization is a force that either must be harnessed in favor of the working class and its allies—or harnessed against us. Fortunately, global solidarity is occurring, as evidenced by the numerous anti-war resolutions sprouting in labor halls. It is also reflected in the fact that only recently the United Steelworkers and International Association of Machinists in the U.S., along with Germany's IG-Metall and Britain's Amicus have banded together in a fledgling alliance of workers. This is an inevitable response to the footloose mobility of capital, which delights in pitting one section of the working class against another—with working class U.S. troops being deployed in Iraq and Afghanistan as the nightmare scenario in that regard.[58]

Still, this worker solidarity ultimately must take the form of independent political action in the interests of labor. Japan provides one clear example. For there in this nation of 110 million, there is a Communist Party with almost 400,000 members, organized in 26,000 branches, with a newspaper with a circulation of 500,000 daily and 2 million on Sunday—larger than *The New York Times*, in other words. It is one of the largest opposition parties in the Parliament and continually addresses matters of improved working conditions, health, education—and peace.[59] As a partial result, universal health care reigns in Japan, while on this side of the Pacific, tens of millions are bereft of basic medical care.

More than a century ago, W.E.B. Du Bois proclaimed that the problem of the 20th Century is the problem of the "color line." As a new century unfolds, his aphorism has not lost resonance, although today it is possible to add the important footnote that the remedy for the problem he delineated rests with international worker solidarity, particularly targeting U.S. imperialism, the land of his birth. In the following pages, I will provide a portrait of this phenomenon that—it is to be hoped—will aid immeasurably those involved in resistance to the depredations of U.S. imperialism.

1: The Business of War

Osama Bin Laden was sick.

It was July 2001 and the heir to a major Saudi fortune, who had fought shoulder to shoulder with U.S. allies in Afghanistan, had made his way to a U.S. hospital in steamy Dubai for medical care. He checked into this 100-bed acute care general hospital—ironically on the 4th of July—and befitting a millionaire, luxuriated there for ten days before departing. He had arrived from Quetta, Pakistan, which was the base from which the CIA had so successfully aided the destabilization of Afghanistan, and was accompanied by an entourage that included his personal physician and a top aide. There, propped up in bed, he greeted a steady stream of local dignitaries, family members—and according to the conservative *Washington Times*, reporting days after 9/11, citing the equally conservative French journal, *Le Figaro*—a "local CIA agent."

Why would a CIA agent meet with a man who already had been designated an enemy of Washington, accused of being implicated in the bombing of U.S. embassies in Kenya and Tanzania three years earlier, not to mention a fatal attack on a U.S. battleship in Yemeni waters in the Fall of 2000? Why would a U.S. official commune with a man sworn to undermine the Saudi regime, a major purchaser of U.S. Treasury debt and a chief supplier of that precious fluid known as petroleum?

Old habits die hard. The Saudi mastermind had been a valuable asset to Washington in fighting their mutual foe—the Communist influenced left—and though he was thought to be alienated from the royal family in his homeland, there were those among the U.S. ruling elite who remained close to his family, as evidenced by the curious fact that many of his close relatives were flown out of the U.S. not long after the murder of civilians in lower Manhattan. Moreover, the "two track foreign policy" long had been a specialty in Washington—smiles and embraces publicly, undermining behind the scenes: look at U.S. relations with Mozambique during the 1980s, for example. Such an approach has the virtue—from U.S. imperialism's viewpoint—of softening up a nation, making it more susceptible to Washington's blandishments. Certainly U.S. imperialism's relationship with Riyadh is exceedingly complicated, as evidenced by the curious 6 August 2002 leak to the *Washington Post* which indicated that this regime was depicted as an "enemy" of the U.S. in official briefings.

French authorities suggested that the meeting in Dubai may have concerned his sharing "information regarding future terrorist strikes" by those not in his circle—there is no honor among thieves, after all. Similarly curious is the fact that days after the Dubai confab, a group that was alleged to have been plotting to blow up the U.S. Embassy in Paris were arrested.[1]

Of course, the CIA dismissed the report as a "total absurdity"[2]—but in Washington-speak, that is virtually an admission that there was something to the story since they did not say that the story was "false" or a "lie." Stung, Radio France International went a step further and identified the CIA agent as "Larry Mitchell," one of the agency's key operatives in the Arab world, with a history in dirty tricks that would put George Clooney's character in "Syriana" to shame. The *Washington Times* reported speculation that as late as the reported July 2001 meeting, the CIA continued to view Bin Laden as a prodigal son—or a close relative that one would not isolate just because he had totaled your car, burned down your house, looted your bank accounts and murdered your spouse.

After all, the stakes were incredibly high and whatever his depredations, Bin Laden was not thought to represent a challenge to the prerogatives of capital—unlike those he had fought in Afghanistan. A few months after the reported July 2001 meeting, *Agence France Presse* provided further context, citing the sage words of Ahmed Rashid, author and analyst, who noted that it was "clear" that U.S. imperialism had been supporting the Taliban in Afghanistan—Bin Laden's close ally. Speaking in October 2001, he observed that "The United States encouraged Saudi Arabia and Pakistan to support the Taliban, certainly right up to their advance on Kabul" in September 1996.

Why?

As this Paris-based news agency put it, "Keen to see Afghanistan under strong central rule to allow a U.S.-led group to build a multi-billion dollar oil and gas pipeline, Washington urged key allies Pakistan and Saudi Arabia to back the militia's bid for power in 1996......the California-based Unocal Corp. in 1996 hatched plans to stretch the pipeline from the Central Asian state of Turkmenistan to Pakistan and the United States and the oil consortium wanted most of Afghanistan to be under the stable control of one government to ensure the pipeline's security..." The Taliban had the virtue, as Washington saw it, of being able to neutralize rival warlords that had carved up the nation. This maneuvering had the added benefit—from the viewpoint of U.S. imperialism—of isolating the nemesis that Iran was thought to be, which had mooted a rival pipeline deal.[3]

Moreover, Washington owed a debt of gratitude to the Taliban because of its critical role in dislodging the late leftist leader of Afghanistan: Najibullah. Along with the bloodthirsty maniac, Gulbuddin Hekmatyar, Washington managed to overthrow this Moscow-backed leader and his feminist reforms that were then squashed by homicidal and male chauvinist fanatics. The scholar, Juan Cole, is one of the few who recalls the unfortunate 1986 episode when Senator Orrin Hatch of Utah, Fred Ikle and other Reagan Administration officials flew to Beijing to plead with China to intercede with its close friend Pakistan to allow the U.S. to give Hekmatyar and other lunatics Stinger anti-aircraft missiles to use against the left in Afghanistan. Islamabad was compelled to acquiesce. Today all of these missiles have yet to be accounted for—and this provides a mortal threat to any flying civilian aircraft. Thus, by November 2001 one of these powerful weapons was found outside Prince Sultan airbase in Saudi Arabia, where it apparently had been fired at a U.S. jet without apparent effect. Shortly thereafter Washington was worrying about Hekmatyar's armed threat to their puppet regime in Kabul.[4]

It was left to the thoughtful writer, Alexander Cockburn, who— weeks after 9/11—cited a damning State Department memorandum from the Summer of 1979 that pointed out that "the United States' larger interest would be served by the demise of the [Moscow-backed] regime, despite whatever setbacks this might mean for future social and economic reforms in Afghanistan." [5]

And in a repetition of a trans-national pattern—that also has afflicted neighborhoods and communities right here in the U.S.—as the left was forced to retreat, filling the resultant vacuum were various forms of ultranationalism.[6]

There was also a regional pattern of long-standing. The writer, Robert Dreyfuss, observes that as early as the 1950s, then U.S. President Dwight D. Eisenhower was conferring with so-called "Islamic fundamentalists" about their mutual antipathy to the organized left. Originally, part of the value of Saddam Hussein to U.S. imperialism was his hard-nosed approach toward Iraqi Communists. Once it was thought that Shi'a Islam was a front for Communist parties, with Iraq pointed to as evidence—but when U.S. imperialism had completed its dirty work, this religious grouping, which had been once seen as a tribune for the oppressed, was viewed quite differently.[7]

Over a quarter century ago there was much discussion about the so-called "October Surprise," whereby the presidential campaign of then GOP candidate Ronald W. Reagan conferred with emissaries of Ayatollah Khomeni of Iran about delaying the release of U.S. hostages in Teheran until after the November 1980 election. They were promptly released on the day of Reagan's inauguration, which provided a massive psychological boost to this fledgling administration. Prior to that Teheran and Washington had collaborated in squashing a mutual foe—the Tudeh Party, i.e. Iranian Communists. The "Iran-Contra" scandal of the mid-1980s demonstrated once more the abject collaboration between conservative hawks in Washington and so-called "Islamic fundamentalists" in Teheran.[8]

In sum, U.S. imperialism was more than willing to accept the medieval oppression that the Taliban was to bring, in return for the promise of access to vast energy resources. Washington was willing to play Russian Roulette with the lives of ordinary Afghanis—what they did not expect was the speeding bullet that came their way on September 11th, thanks to their former friends in Kabul. "The Taliban will probably develop like the Saudis did," said an unnamed U.S. official in 1997. "There will be Aramco [the former U.S. oil consortium in Saudi Arabia], pipelines, an emir, no parliament and lots of Sharia law. We can live with that," he said, oblivious of the lives to be snuffed out in Manhattan four years later.[9]

This ho-hum attitude toward those who were shortly to be regarded as fearsome "terrorists" was an outgrowth of a conscious U.S. policy of collaborating with these cutthroats in order to destabilize the global left. But Afghanistan is simply a global prototype. For example, during the 1990s U.S. imperialism wanted to raise a "jihadi corps" to aid their allies in Bosnia—once a part of Socialist Yugoslavia. According to *The Guardian* of London, Pakistan—then led by Benazir Bhutto—dispatched a contingent there (at the behest of the Clinton White House). This group was formed from the Harkut-ul-Ansar, trained by the notorious intelligence service of Islamabad—who, of course, were essential in the collaboration with Osama Bin Laden that characterized the war in neighboring Afghanistan. It turns out that this "jihadi corps" was recruited in Britain itself from the sizeable Pakistani community there, shedding new light on why London has been wracked with "terrorist" assaults of late. Further, Washington gave a green light to Hezbollah, the Lebanese grouping that bested Israel in the Summer 2006—and is now ritualistically denounced as "terrorist"—to join the "jihadi corps" in Bosnia. Simultaneously, U.S. imperialism assisted Islamist insurgents linked to Chechnya—thereby angering Moscow, and Iran (now an official member of the "axis of evil") as well as Saudi Arabia in the successful attempt to destroy Socialist Yugoslavia.

Omar Saeed Sheikh, the man now in prison in Pakistan for murdering *Wall Street Journal* reporter Daniel Pearl—whose slaying was the subject of an affecting Hollywood movie starring Angelina Jolie—was a leader of this "jihadi corps" that was dispatched successfully to Socialist

Yugoslavia. This is the same Omar Saeed Sheikh who, at the behest of Pakistani intelligence wired $100,000 to Mohammed Atta, the leading 9/11 hijacker and mass murderer, just before the attack on Manhattan. *The Guardian* was astonished that the "official 9/11 Commission Report of July 2004," not only "sought to downplay the role of Pakistan" but, perhaps worse, did not seek to investigate the likes of Omar Saeed Sheikh.[10]

Sadly, few in the U.S. have come to recognize the critical collaboration between U.S. imperialism and those now routinely denounced as "terrorists." This collaboration was so important—and so recent—it has not received the critical attention it merits, not least because it would be so discrediting to those who continue to exercise power and influence. After all, these "terrorists" and their handiwork in Afghanistan and Bosnia were instrumental in the accomplishment of what U.S. imperialism considers to be one of its primary attainments—the ouster of Communist parties in Eastern Europe. The inextricable tie between what is now said to be a chief threat to national security ("terrorism") and its foremost accomplishment (the so-called "death of communism") has prevented a searching and honest excavation of 9/11 and, indeed, U.S. imperialism as a whole.

This perilous combination of amnesia and laryngitis when it comes to analyzing the historic collaboration between so-called "Islamic fundamentalism" and U.S. imperialism reaches the height of absurdity when it comes to examining Saudi Arabia, a nation on which Main Street and Wall Street have become dependent, not least for oil and financing of public and private debt. Youseff Ibrahim, a former reporter for *The New York Times*, has found Bush's policy toward this regime "baffling"—and it is: until one considers this dependency and the closer than lips and teeth relationship that has emerged between the leading feudal and imperialist regimes. Still, Ibrahim could not understand why there had not been more scrutiny of Sulaiman Al-Rajhi, a reclusive Saudi octogenarian with a personal fortune of $12 billion and his own Islamic bank with 500 branches in his homeland. For decades—stretching back to the 1980s war in Afghanistan—he has served as a conduit, financier and facilitator for "Al Qaeda" and like-minded groupings. He is not alone in his sympathies. The majority of suicide bombers in contemporary Iraq are of Saudi origin, as are 40% of the foreign fighters. As he examined the details, Ibrahim found it hard to determine if what was involved was "Bush's unbridled naivete" or the more technical—and explosive—charge of his "'collaborating with the enemy.'" [11]

Actually, neither suspicion is altogether accurate. Like many U.S. nationals, Ibrahim has difficulty slicing through the hubristic national chauvinism to recognize that the self-proclaimed "sole remaining superpower" is in a dire crisis, which is manifested in its dangerous and historic dependence upon a feudal regime. Just as Pakistan has a dangerous dependence upon U.S. imperialism and is thereby constrained when the powerful in Washington muse about overthrowing the regime, U.S. imperialism has found itself handcuffed in confronting Riyadh, not only due to oil and purchasing of debt but also because key members of the Saudi royal family are key investors in important enterprises, not least Citicorp, the premier New York City bank and financial octopus.

Even the *Wall Street Journal*, usually satisfied in playing the dummy to the conservative hawks' ventriloquist, was struck by some of the more recent developments involving Riyadh. Nervously, their columnist, Bret Stephens, recounted the sensitive 2003 episode when it was reported that Al Qaeda had sought "to recruit Saudi Arabian air force pilots to carry out a suicide attack..."[12]

It is apparent that there is a split at the highest levels of the U.S ruling elite as to what to do about Riyadh, with the Bush White House and the conservative hawks that he represents taking a softer line. The problem is that the line of the conservative hawks may have been appropriate for overall ruling elite aims during the titanic struggle against the former Soviet Union but now that line is jeopardizing national survival. The problem is that being rigid ideologues and given their status in certain circles as the embodiment of manliness, the ultimate guardian of white supremacy and the soul of the nation, it is difficult for these hawks to adapt to this new post-Cold War dispensation. The further problem is that we are all aboard a ship heading straight for a massive iceberg with ideologically drunken incompetents at the wheel.

This was the backdrop to the August 2002 leak that described Riyadh as an "enemy" of the U.S. Since 15 of the 19 hijackers on 9/11 were of Saudi origin, this conclusion is understandable. This was no minor matter. At a briefing of the Pentagon's potent Defense Policy Board, chaired by the self-proclaimed "Prince of Darkness," the chubby and graying Richard Perle, Laurent Murawiec of the Rand Corporation was unsparing: "the Saudis," he said, "are active at every level of the terror chain, from planners to financiers, from cadre to foot-soldier, from ideologist to cheerleader." Riyadh, it was announced, "supports our enemies and attacks our allies;" it is "the kernel of evil, the prime mover, the most dangerous opponent." The briefing warned that U.S. imperialism should demand that Riyadh halt its funding of so-called "Islamic fundamentalism" (which would eviscerate the raison d'etre of the regime, akin to a suicide and, therefore, highly unlikely) and "prosecute or isolate those involved in the terror chain, including the Saudi intelligence services." The briefing linked the impending regime change in Iraq with Saudi

Arabia in that once Saddam was overthrown, U.S. imperialism would become less dependent on Saudi oil and give Washington far more latitude in lassoing Riyadh. Evidently the briefing did not acknowledge the tantalizing possibility that a U.S. imperialism in crisis is having the same "two track" foreign policy that it perfected in using against others now—with the tables turned—being deployed against Washington: i.e. Riyadh is at once an "ally" of Washington while acquiescing to those who harbor a sharply opposing viewpoint.

Evidently, the only person present at this briefing that objected was Henry Kissinger, the aging Machiavellian and former Secretary of State. Others present included former Pentagon chiefs, James Schlesinger and Harold Brown; former Vice President Dan Quayle; former House Speakers Thomas Foley and Newt Gingrich; and two former Vice-Chairs of the Joint Chiefs of Staff—retired admirals David Jeremiah and William Owens. Kenneth Adelman, former Reagan Administration official, and a member of the Board did not attend but this enthusiastic backer of the 1980s war in Afghanistan and the invasion of Iraq, disagreed with Kissinger, arguing that Riyadh was indeed an adversary. *The Weekly Standard* of 15 July 2002, a journal controlled by reactionary Australian-American media baron, Rupert Murdoch (the same man who controls the GOP channel, Fox News), echoed the briefing, predicting the "Coming Saudi Showdown." [13]

But whatever visions percolated about dislodging the Saudi monarchy disappeared, like so many other dreams, in the sands of Iraq—apparently. The larger point is that overthrowing this regime, given its essential role in the economy and fortunes of U.S. imperialism could be as disastrous and fraught with complication and unintended consequence as an attempt by Pakistan to overthrow its patron in Washington would be. Not least, it could choke off the lifeblood of U.S. imperialism—petroleum, the key to Washington's policy in the entire region..

Toppling the Riyadh regime may not occur today—but the gnawing unease about this theocracy continues. In July 2007 it was reported that the White House is now wallowing in "frustration" since it "appears that Saudi Arabia has stepped up efforts to undermine the Maliki government" in Baghdad. This frustration is buoyed by an indelicate pronouncement from a Saudi official that his government would intervene decisively in Iraq to bolster its Sunni allies if U.S. imperialism retreated from this conflict. Washington has its own grievance about indelicacy in that in April 2007 King Abdullah condemned the "illegal foreign occupation" of Iraq by U.S. imperialism. From Riyadh's viewpoint, Washington erred disastrously when it removed two of Iran's chief antagonists—Saddam in Baghdad and the Taliban in Kabul—thereby unsettling the region and, potentially, imperiling Saudi Arabia itself. Now the serial blunderers in Washington seek to undo—actually compound—their ill-conceived deeds by threatening Iran.[14]

What is occurring is that akin to many erstwhile friends and antagonists of U.S. imperialism, like a smart shark Riyadh smells blood in the water, sensing the deepening crisis of U.S. imperialism, it is rethinking the relationship and casting about for other bonds of affection; like so many others in this category, their wandering eyes have alit on Beijing, the perceived rising power: Chinese officials have visited Saudi Arabia so frequently in recent months—and vice versa—that the frequent flier miles racked up by both sides could be cashed in profitably. Boxed into a corner, U.S. imperialism can only flail about as its source of capital—a resource recycled from oil sales to the U.S. and elsewhere—inches away.

U.S. imperialism faces a similar dilemma in confronting its erstwhile Cold War ally in Islamabad. Pakistan was essential to the destabilization of the Moscow-backed regime in Afghanistan but finds it difficult today to adjust to Washington's new line that has become more critical of so-called "Islamic fundamentalism." Many of those accused of "terrorist" bombings in Western Europe have direct connections to Islamabad. Pakistan is willing to hand over to the North Atlantic powers some with connections to Al Qaeda but is reluctant to act similarly towards the Taliban, seeing the perpetuation of this force as critical to its long-term plan to develop "strategic depth" in the region, particularly when it comes to confrontation with the eternal foe in New Delhi.

Yet the smashing of the regional left during the Cold War— Najibullah in Kabul, the Tudeh Party in Teheran, etc.—means that U.S. imperialism has choices between bad and worse alternatives when it comes to contemplating regime change in Riyadh and Islamabad.

This cataclysmic situation could not be occurring at a worse moment for U.S. imperialism, for it compels it to be more adventurous than usual in seeking possible replacements for Riyadh most notably. For as the U.S. invasion of Afghanistan was gaining momentum, even *The New York Times*, typically decorous in avoiding the seamy details of the lust for oil that underpins U.S. foreign policy, felt compelled to respond. "Skeptics, especially in the Islamic world," their readers were informed belatedly on 15 December 2001, "contend that oil interests lie at the heart of the West's war in Afghanistan. 'The Pipeline is Greed,' read the headline in a recent article in the Pakistani newspaper '*Dawn*' about the American-led attacks on the Taliban and Al Qaeda. 'The war on terrorism may well be a war for resources,' it said."

Perhaps what motivated this rare burst of candor unleashed on *Times'* readers was the unavoidable fact that then Secretary of State Colin

L. Powell had just returned from a visit to Kazakhstan in Central Asia, not far distant from Afghanistan—part of the bounty claimed by U.S. oil giants after the Soviet Union's collapse; the former General was "particularly impressed," it was said "with the money that American oil companies were investing there. He estimated that $200 billion could flow into Kazakhstan during the next 5 to 10 years." But a possible cloud on an otherwise rainbow of optimism was the gathering hostility that was espied in a resurgent Moscow, which was digging itself out of the rubble brought by the disastrous reign of Boris Yeltsin and was doing so on the basis of gushing revenues from oil and gas fields. "In the last year, the attitude of Russian oil companies to Western ones has changed," said Yevgeny Khartukov, General Director of the International Center for Petroleum Business Studies, a nonprofit research and consulting group in Moscow. "Now they don't need them." Among other things, the U.S. war in Afghanistan forcefully reasserted Washington's presence in a region overflowing with oil and natural gas.[15]

In brief, it would be one-sided to see the U.S. war in Afghanistan as being solely triggered by the desire for oil and gas, but it would be naïve to assume that these resources were irrelevant when the time arrived to launch an invasion.

Like *Dawn* in neighboring Pakistan, India's press was also quite skeptical about the intervention of U.S. imperialism in Afghanistan, aware as they were of the previous snuggly relationship between the Taliban and certain elements in Washington. "Afghanistan occupies the central position in the U.S strategy for the economic control of the oil and gas resources in the entire Middle East," claimed a writer in *The Hindu* on 13 October 2001. "The U.S. currently imports 51 percent of its crude oil— 19.5 million barrels daily. The Energy Information Administration estimates that by 2020, the U.S. will import 64 percent of its crude—25.8 million barrels a day. Caspian oil reserves might be third largest in the world (after Western Siberia and the Persian Gulf) and within the next 15 to 20 years, may be large enough to offset Persian Gulf oil... Caspian Sea oil and gas are not the only hydrocarbon deposits in the region. Turkmenistan's Karakum Desert holds the world's third largest gas reserves—three trillion cubic meters—and has six billion barrels of estimated oil reserves. Current estimates indicate that, in addition to huge deposits, the Caspian basin may hold as much as 200 billion barrels of oil—33 times the estimated holdings of Alaska's North Slope and a current value of $4 trillion. It is enough to meet the U.S.' energy needs for 30 years or more."[16]

It was in 1995 with these visions of super-profits dancing merrily like sugar-plums in their heads that Unocal started negotiating to build oil and gas pipelines from Turkmenistan, through Afghanistan and into

Pakistani ports on the Arabian Sea—a deal that required getting in bed with the Taliban.[17] This affair with the Taliban would have been consummated—but for the angry intervention of U.S. feminists (including Mavis Leno, the spouse of the late-night comedian) which compelled Washington to be seen to place some daylight between itself and the medievalists.

This reality was generally submerged in the aftermath of the attack on Manhattan, yet occasionally it managed to peek through. Some Washingtonians—particularly those who reside at 1600 Pennsylvania Avenue—may have gagged on their morning coffee when they espied CNN's Paula Zahn interviewing the former U.N. Weapons Inspector Richard Butler, on 8 January 2002. The balding, bulky, bespectacled Australian—thought to be a lapdog of Bush, like his Prime Minister, John Howard—instead startled viewers when he announced in his nasal accent that the "administration....just shortly after assuming office slowed down FBI investigations of Al Qaeda and terrorism in Afghanistan in order to do a deal with the Taliban on oil—an oil pipeline across Afghanistan.." Butler thought this was worthy of further investigation but, quite typically, that bright idea emerged stillborn.[18]

Now Washington has installed successfully the puppet regime in Kabul led by Hamid Karzai, though the Taliban—which was boosted when the left was smashed—has yet to be squashed, though thousands of NATO troops have joined the fight. Opium production is reaching record highs and corruption is rampant. Today the U.S. is now bogged down in Afghanistan, along with its increasingly restive NATO allies. The nation is a mess. The Taliban and its Al Qaeda allies have regained territory, while violent attacks on the U.S. and its allies are routine. In Kabul, thought to be a redoubt for the U.S. backed regime, things are so dangerous that foreign embassies are in a state of lockdown, diplomats do not leave their offices—unless accompanied by small platoons in armored vehicles. The situation is worse for U.S. personnel, since for them Afghanistan is a prison.[19]

Actually, Kabul's chief anti-corruption fighter, Izzatullah Wasifi, once spent years in a Nevada prison after being nabbed with millions of dollars in heroin. One of Karzai's close relatives is said to be a major player in the flourishing drug business in Kandahar, while Wasifi has been a lifelong friend of the Afghan leader whose actual remit barely reaches beyond his office in Kabul.[20]

The problem for U.S. imperialism—regionally, globally, politically, and economically—is that this system of craven plunder spent trillions to subdue the former Soviet Union, not least due to the perceived threat it sensed from a socialist community animated by the notion of constructing a strong public sector. Now in the aftermath of this gigantic "victory," Washington awakens to the reality that this "threat" has yet to be extirpated in that it now has to contend with "Sovereign Wealth Funds" directed by the state and oil companies controlled by the state. With regard to the former there is grave concern that they will avoid increasingly discredited U.S. securities in favor of more tangible investments—like banks, manufacturers and the like. With regard to the latter, privately owned U.S. giants e.g. Exxon-Mobil, have grumbled about competing against foreign oil giants that are state owned since their chief motivation is not necessarily profit or quarterly return on investment. This gives these U.S. rivals more flexibility in terms of cutting deals or even making long-term exploration and investment plans.

According to *Le Monde Diplomatique*, "77% of the world's hydrocarbons are owned" by "National Oil Companies....therefore by the public sector." This is not trivial. Exxon-Mobil "had a turnover of $370 billion in 2005 ($450 billion in 2006, according to Wall Street estimates), more than the GDP of 195 members of the United Nations" but feels threatened by these "NOCs." Worsening relations between Washington and Moscow has been the latter's snatching back oil concessions allocated by the Yeltsin clique to the privately controlled Royal Dutch Shell. The government's stake in the old Soviet gas industry had fallen to "only 38% in the 10 years after its privatization in 1992, the majority of its capital having been creamed off by Yeltsin's Prime Minister and his cronies." The directors of Gazprom (the resultant Russian oil and gas giant) "mislaid an average of $2 billion every year, along with 10% of reserves." June 2000 can be marked as the beginning of Washington's alienation from Moscow for that is when President Vladimir Putin "put his own man in charge of Gazprom, which controls 25%, maybe even 33% of the planet's natural gas reserves. In December 2005 the state became the majority shareholder with 51% of the company's capital" as "Gazprom recovered its assets" from the plunderers. In a sense, President Putin clawed back a major chunk of U.S. imperialism's Cold War victory over the former Soviet Union by seeking to reinstall the remit of the state.[21]

A prickly bone of contention between Washington and Venezuela is precisely this issue of the latitude displayed by the latter's state-owned oil company, which is now widening its challenge to U.S. imperialism by collaborating with a similarly situated Iran in producing inexpensive automobiles and tractors, thereby challenging yet another sphere that has been dominated by the North Atlantic powers.

In other words, the bellicosity in Washington cannot be divorced from the desperation of U.S. imperialism, impelled to go for broke by both grabbing a major source of petroleum in Iraq and a potential site for a pipeline in Afghanistan, in the face of stiff challenges from state-owned oil companies that are reviving the worst Cold War nightmares. This desperation also illuminates Washington's remarkable tolerance of Saudi Arabia, which routinely puts a thumb in the eye of U.S. imperialism, but is difficult to bash because of its role as a source of oil in a world where regimes like Venezuela, Iran and Russia are rapidly attaining hegemony in this field and are more than willing to collaborate with China and other rising powers, to Washington's dismay.

Indeed, at times it seems that the U.S. government and, at times, the nation itself, exists to serve the interests of oil companies. This perception is — pardon the expression — fueled by the growing reality that the Pentagon increasingly seems to be in business to gain control over oil supplies that allows it to pursue its dirty dreams. The progressive writer, Michael Klare, pointed out that the average U.S. soldier in Iraq and Afghanistan consumes on a daily basis 16 gallons of oil — either directly through the use of Humvees, tanks, trucks and helicopters, or indirectly by calling in air strikes. This amounts to a gargantuan 3.5 million gallons of oil expended daily in these war zones alone. This does not count the millions more expended in the scores of far-flung U.S. military bases. A mere two years ago the U.S. Department of Energy predicted confidently that the price of crude oil would hover in the $30 a barrel range — well, it passed that limit rather quickly and is now heading for $90. Just as government borrowing to fund the Pentagon may be crowding out investment in more fruitful and productive arenas, the military's covetousness when it comes to oil may be helping to drive up the price at the pump, not to mention home-heating oil, fuel for commercial airplanes and the like. This is occurring as some analysts are forecasting an era of "peak oil" or the probability that the sources for oil may be drying up, a signal factor in propelling the drive for solar power, bio-fuels, wind-power and the like. In the meantime, this dramatically changing scenario sheds light on why U.S. imperialism — and the Pentagon — focuses so intently on the Persian Gulf, the mother lode of oil, a "service" it provides for U.S. corporations e.g. General Motors and Boeing, whose future fortunes are heavily dependent upon the price of oil. But this is also a matter of survival for the Pentagon itself, particularly when one considers that during the 1991 Gulf War, the average soldier expended about 4 gallons of oil daily. Thus, the Pentagon's use of oil is expanding as the known global supply is declining — this too impels the swashbuckling belligerence of U.S. imperialism.[22]

Thus, the desire to smash the Baathist regime in Baghdad was a turnabout from the Cold War era when Washington dispatched Donald Rumsfeld to shake hands with Saddam Hussein and further weaken Iraq and Iran — to the benefit of the privately owned oil companies — as they engaged in mutual bloodletting. The collapse of the Soviet Union altered the global calculus. The merger of these two trends can be witnessed in the person of former Soviet citizen, Dr. Ken Alibek, who migrated to the U.S. and became a major expert arguing that Saddam had weapons of mass destruction. In return he obtained $28 million in federal grants for his various enterprises. It was perversely appropriate that a remnant of the Cold War like Alibek helped to lead U.S. imperialism into the debacle that has become Iraq.[23]

*   *   *

Of course, George W. Bush has to tread lightly when it comes to the ultra-sensitive matter of the oil industry and the ramified ties between business and government. A man who points proudly to his roots in this industry and his role with Arbusto Energy, not to mention personally selecting a Vice-President with similar ties, has to be careful in bringing attention to this gushing fountain of profits. After all, his father, the former President, has a similar background, and during the early years of his son's presidency captured headlines with his prominent role in the Carlyle Group, which happened to have massive investments in industries that could rise or fall depending upon the maneuvers of the occupant of the White House — something that "Uncle Bucky" could testify about personally. This private equity firm, which revealed its role as exemplar of state monopoly capitalism by placing its headquarters in Washington, D.C. — and not Wall Street — was worth a hefty $12 billion by early 2001. It also included Bush family consigliere, James A. Baker III, the former Secretary of State and Secretary of the Treasury; former British Prime Minister John Major and former President of the Philippines, Fidel Ramos — an indication of its global pretensions. Even during the earliest days of the administration of Bush the lesser, it was regarded as one of the nation's biggest defense contractors and a force in global telecommunications. Investors in Carlyle have included major banks and insurance companies, pension funds and wealthy investors from Dubai to Singapore.

Carlyle has been very, very good to the Bush family. Recall that it was in 1990 when the younger Bush was a recovering alcoholic and a bust in business that this mega-firm tossed him a life raft and placed him on the board of their subsidiary, Caterair, an airline-catering company. By the time Bush entered the White House, Carlyle had become a colossus with stakes in 164 companies, which last year employed more than 70,000 people. Interestingly, it has become one of the nation's major defense contractors and, therefore, bound to benefit from the installation of a warmonger in the White House. Given that George W. Bush is ineluctably a major beneficiary of the family wealth generated by George H.W. Bush, this situation—minimally—appeared to be quite unseemly.[24]

For example, as the conflict in Afghanistan was being launched and planning for war in Iraq was accelerated, on a single day during this period Carlyle earned a princely $237 million selling shares in United Defense Industries, the Army's fifth largest contractor. This profiteering has attracted some strange bedfellows. The company owned by the fabulously affluent Bin Laden family of Saudi Arabia, not willing to miss out on a good bet invested $2 million in Carlyle—not a bad hedging strategy in that they would be in clover irrespective of who prevailed in the "war against terror." (In fairness, this investment seems to have been liquidated—after 11 September 2001.)[25]

State monopoly capitalism today is characterized by a sinful circle that unites an expansionist imperialist ideology—or "neo-conservatism"—shameless profiteering and influence peddling at the highest levels. The business publications where the shilling minds of the elite meet are "Exhibit A" in this regard. "Why Defense Stocks are Going Great Guns" chortled *Business Week* in August 2000—prematurely, but tellingly—anticipating the contested election of George W. Bush. While ordinary stock indexes were up 7.3% in the months leading to their gleeful reporting, "Litton Industries has rocketed 103%, Lockheed Martin has soared 79%, Northrop Grumman has risen 84%, and General Dynamics is up 73%."[26]

In such an atmosphere it is not surprising that the now disgraced and jailed former Congressman Randy "Duke" Cunningham sold his vote to the highest (military) bidder; theretofore, he had been known—surprise, surprise—as a fierce conservative hawk. Receiving less publicity was the story of David H. Safavian, the Bush Administration official—who was arrested in the late summer of 2005 on charges of obstructing the investigation of the corrupt power-broker, Jack Abramoff (previously this dedicated anticommunist was notorious for producing a Hollywood movie in apartheid occupied Namibia, which touted the bona fides of the Angolan mass murderer, Jonas Savimbi). In the aftermath of Safavian's discrediting, it emerged that he had links to suspected terrorist organizations. He was also a registered foreign agent for Gabon, an African nation whose human rights violations make the press' frequent whipping boy—Zimbabwe—pale into insignificance. He was also a lobbyist for Pakistan and toiled tirelessly for the Northern Marianas Islands—the U.S. colony in the South Seas—when it sought to block the imposition of the minimum wage.[27]

Though conservatives have prattled and prated endlessly about "getting the government off the backs of the people," they failed to indicate what they really intended was sticking their paws into the government's pocket.

Thus, it was not surprising when a *Business Week* headline crowed in February, 2002—a scant year before the catastrophic invasion of Iraq: "Striking Saddam: Some Stocks Could Soar." The analyst, Byron Callan, at the well-connected Wall Street firm, Merrill Lynch, informed the investor class that "A U.S. military campaign to oust Saddam Hussein's regime should benefit companies that produce 'military consummables'," e.g. ammunition and spare parts. Thus, he expected certain stocks to reach stratospheric heights, including Alliant Techsystems, Raytheon, and L3 Communications. The company that makes Tomahawk cruise missiles and "precision-guided weapons used in naval and air strikes" was expected to see its stock price fly as high as its product. The demented desires of the more rapacious investors were vindicated when the illegal and criminal invasion of Iraq was commenced in March 2003 with precisely a rocket attack against a site near the center of Baghdad where Saddam Hussein and company had been reported to be presiding.

The invasion of Iraq may have been geo-political disaster, a criminal enterprise, the biggest foreign policy catastrophe in the history of U.S. imperialism—and worse—but, as it turned out, *Business Week* was accurate in forecasting that it would be a bonanza for Big Business. In fact, these two sharply differing outcomes may very well be connected in that the invasion and occupation was plotted as an exercise in validating a key principle of conservative-think: privatization; The problem is that a soldier salutes and executes—by law—while a privateer may flee when faced with less than satisfactory conditions, a euphemism for what now exists in Iraq. In the vain pursuit of profit, U.S. imperialism has compromised a central principle of military science—the importance of a unified command and control.

There are now nearly as many private contractors in Iraq as there are U.S. soldiers. They operate with little or no supervision, accountable only to the firms employing them. They have been accused of worsening an already parlous situation by not only slaying an undetermined number of Iraqi nationals but also firing indiscriminately at not only Iraqi but U.S. troops as well. Security firms alone have earned billions, while worsening military morale since their employees earn much, much more than ordinary soldiers. The chief culprit, Blackwater, is located in the Deep South—bastion of the most retrograde conservatism—and it reflects the region where it is sited; it also has secured about a billion dollars in contracts in Iraq.[28] KBR, with historic ties to Vice President Cheney's former employer, Halliburton, is also located in the South—Texas in this case— and similarly has profited handsomely from this failed Iraqi adventure. EOD Technology, also is located in the South—Tennessee—and in Iraq has supplied security and explosives.[29]

KBR notwithstanding, Blackwater has become the poster child for the lucrative business of war. Erik Prince, the crew cut, boyish former Navy Seal, who founded the company, was a White House intern under George H.W. Bush and has been a GOP financier since, chalking up $225,000 in contributions. His sister, Betsy DeVos, is a former chair of the Michigan Republican Party; her spouse, Richard DeVos, was the GOP nominee for Governor in that state in 2006.Blackwater has received $1 billion in federal contracts; it charges the government $1222 per day for each operative it dispatches to Iraq—more than 6 times the wage of an equivalent soldier.[30]

Such is the apotheosis of modern conservatism: Imperialist ideology fueling foreign invasions grounded in a bankrupt ideology of privatization, with profits being directed heavily toward firms in the South, the former headquarters of African slavery and the current headquarters of reactionary politicos. Digging ourselves out of the hole prepared for us by conservatism will require a vigorous attack on every link of this chain, starting with the South. But it will also require a recognition that what has contributed to U.S. imperialism's crisis—which has metastasized into a crisis for the nation—is the Cold War onslaught against the organized left globally. This crusade, in the first place, warped the political discourse in the U.S. itself, making it more likely that the inane and bloody plans hatched in Washington would take flight; it also meant that instead of spending on education and health care, these two priorities have been left to wither as Pentagon spending skyrockets.

2: THE AGONY OF WAR

As a result of the criminal and illegal invasion of Iraq by U.S. imperialism, two million in that nation have become refugees eking out a barebones existence in nations near and far, while two million more have been uprooted and remain "internally displaced" in their homeland. Most Iraqis have electricity for only about five hours a day—if they're lucky—while clean water remains scarce. The prize to be seized—Iraqi oil—is produced at a fraction of pre-war levels. Unemployment is at stratospheric levels of 40%. Hundreds of thousands of Iraqis have lost their lives as a result of this war, while about 30,000 U.S. nationals have been killed or maimed.[1]

Under U.S. domination, Iraq has become a charnel house of bones and blood; according to a recent report from Oxfam and a network of aid agencies, based on data from the United Nations, the International Committee of the Red Cross and related agencies,[2] the level of deprivation in Iraq beggars belief.

This has occurred as Iraqi wealth has been stolen and otherwise wasted. The United Nations had amassed a fortune in Iraq oil proceeds and seized bank accounts to the tune of $37 billion, most of it stashed in a Federal Reserve Bank in New York. The Bush Administration demanded custody of this wealth and with the approval of U.N. Resolution 1483, passed in October 2005, the Development Fund for Iraq was created and placed under the White House's Viceroy in Baghdad, L. Paul 'Jerry' Bremer. Soon loads of cash began arriving in Baghdad on giant C-17 cargo planes. Pallets with stacked $100 bills were unloaded, trucked to the capital and then dispatched around Iraq to pay the bills—or whatever. In all, $12 billion in U.S. currency was flown into Iraq before a banking system was set up to handle wire transfers of funds. In all, 363 tons of cash were shipped. And as a congressional investigation demonstrated, a good deal of this Iraqi money simply disappeared. Thus, in January 2005, Stuart Bower, Jr., appointed by Congress to investigate this fiasco, could not verify that $8.8 billion turned over to Iraqi ministries was properly spent. Naturally, Halliburton—the Vice President's company—was involved, receiving $1.6 billion from this cache: overcharging by hundreds of millions of dollars.[3]

Mournfully, this collapse was occurring even before the occupation, as the punishing sanctions imposed by Washington exacted a heavy toll. There is evidence to suggest that as early as August 2001 Washington—contrary to the Geneva Convention—intentionally used sanctions against Iraq to degrade the nation's water supply. This had a devastating impact on Iraqi children particularly. This was done through hampering the importation of specialized equipment and some chemicals to purify its water supply, most of which is heavily mineralized and frequently brackish to saline. Ultimately, the United Nations concluded that as a result of these sanctions alone, some 500,000 Iraqi children perished.[4] It was such malfeasance that spurred the *Washington Post* to blare—well before 11 September 2001—that "U.S. Loses Clout in Arab World." Simon Karem, a former Lebanese Ambassador to the U.S.—again, speaking *before* 9/11—asserted that "the way political events are unfolding, [Washington] is playing into the hands of the bin Ladens." The policy of U.S. imperialism in the region, said the Jordanian newspaper, *Al-Dustur*, "boils down to 'Israel and oil,'" with the weakening of Iraq essential to this strategy in that it has been a leading oil producer while remaining "the one country rich enough and radical enough to challenge 'Israel and oil.'"[5]

It is this state of affairs that calls into question the ostensible rationale for the invasion—i.e. weapons of mass destruction. For it was on 7 January 1999—a full four years before the invasion—that *The New York Times* front-page headline blared, "U.S. Spied on Iraq Under U.N. Cover, Officials Now Say." That is to say, U.S. spies—supposedly U.N. weapons inspectors—inspected Iraq closely in search of weapons. Later the *Hartford Courant*[6] pointed out that these operatives also planted eavesdropping devices throughout the nation. Subsequently, in the weeks preceding the March 2003 invasion, Hans Blix of the U.N. could not confirm the presence of weapons of mass destruction—yet the invasion preceded anyway, raising searching questions if "oil and Israel," as the critics charged, were the real reasons for what has turned out be a catastrophic invasion and occupation.

Now Iraq is fragmenting, its wealth dissipating and many of its nationals ensnared in sectarian strife rather than confronting Israel—to that extent, the invasion and occupation has been a "success." Yet, this disaster for Iraqis may very well prove to be similarly problematic for U.S. imperialism. For as Iraq fragments, the radical autonomy now being pursued by Kurdistan is worrisome to neighboring Turkey, which has a restive Kurdish minority not adverse to armed struggle; already Ankara has crossed the border more than once—which may be a harbinger of a larger invasion. Saudi Arabia has warned that if the U.S. is forced out of Iraq, Riyadh may intervene to protect its own interests and Sunni co-religionists, which could spur a similar maneuver from Iran concerned about the fate of the Shi'a. Moreover, the Saudi oilfields are sited in regions with sizeable Shi'a minorities, which is of no small concern to Riyadh.

U.S. imperialism, which played so assiduously on differences between and among Serbs, Croats, Bosnians and others in order to destroy Socialist Yugoslavia, has not been missing in action in the process that has exacerbated sectarian tensions in Iraq. This supposition was confirmed when the White House indicated that it would press ahead with building a three-mile wall between Sunni and Shi'a neighborhoods in Baghdad, despite the objections of the Iraqi government—not to mention the vehement and vociferous dissent expressed by ordinary Iraqis.[7]

But just as the similarly disastrous invasion and occupation of Vietnam was defeated not least due to angry opposition from countless U.S. nationals—soldiers not least—a similar phenomenon is occurring in Iraq. In a maneuver that stunned official Washington in early 2007, a group of active-duty military personnel and reservists, including many who have served in Iraq, denounced the war and demanded that Congress promptly withdraw the troops. Numbering 1600, this lengthy list included enlisted soldiers in the Army from the lowest to the highest ranks. Specialist Lindsay Burnett who served in Iraq with the First Brigade combat team of the 101st Airborne Division, based at Fort Campbell on the border between Kentucky and Tennessee, expressed the sentiments when he spoke of "a sense of betrayal" spreading among the corps—and growing anger directed toward those at the top. Noteworthy is the fact that about 70% of those signing the petition are on active duty.[8]

Also suggestive of growing unrest in the ranks is the fact that 3196 active-duty soldiers deserted the Army last year—out of 500,000 within the ranks in toto. There is a faster acceleration in the rate of desertions over the previous two fiscal years—even though Army data does not reflect deserters from the 63,000 currently activated National Guard and Reserve soldiers. This is considered to be extraordinary and is linked to the heavy toll of wartime deployments, e.g. many on their second or third tours of duty in Afghanistan—and Iraq. Actually, these figures—as instructive as they are—may be under-estimates since Pentagon records were said to have been damaged severely as a result of the 11 September attack.[9]

Tragically, the number of military suicides is proliferating. In 2006, 99 suicides were reported in the Army; 30 of those occurred in Iraq or Afghanistan. This is an increase from 2005, which witnessed 87 suicides and 2004, which witnessed 67 suicides.[10]

Then there are those who simply refuse to serve, a trend that has swept the colony that is Puerto Rico like a firestorm. This is reflective of both widespread sentiment—and deft organizing. Under the White House's signature legislation—No Child Left Behind Act of 2001—all schools receiving U.S. federal funding must provide their students' names, addresses and phone numbers to the military unless the child or parents sign an opt-out form. For the last five years the Puerto Rican Independence Party has issued opt-out forms to about 120,000 students on the island and encouraged them to sign. They have been joined by other antiwar groups, including the Coalition of Citizens Against Militarism, meaning that students routinely receive more than one opt-out form. As a result, during the 2003-6 period, a mere 4,957 Puerto Ricans enlisted in the Army or Reserves, or approximately 123 people per 100,000 residents—which is below the average contribution of U.S. states and far below the number in such states as Alabama and Oklahoma, each of which enlists more than 200 men and women per 100,000. Polling data suggests that an inspiring 75% of island residents oppose the war in Iraq.[11]

Puerto Ricans are not alone. According to the *New York Amsterdam News*, which serves Harlem, "the war in Iraq has had a devastating effect on the Army's recruitment of Blacks.....since 2000, African-American enrollment in the Army has declined by close to 40%."[12]

This is occurring as sons and daughters of the elite—generally—have declined to join the military, which suggests the ancient aphorism that a ruling class not willing to defend itself is not worth preserving. Moved to alarm, the Pentagon has devised ever more desperate means in order to find recruits. As of March 2007 the U.S. military included 81,000 teenagers. Its 7,350 17-year olds needed parental consent to enlist. In 2002 almost half of Marine recruits were 17 or 18. A Pentagon survey discovered that "for both males and females, propensity [to enlist] is highest among 16 and 17 year olds." That "propensity" declines rapidly with age. But the military aims even lower, marketing itself to children as young as 13 with videos, school visits and cold calls to their homes and mobile phones. In Junior ROTC, kids get uniforms, win medals, fire real guns and play soldier, while adults trained in psychological manipulation steer them toward the army. These manipulators take advantage of the fact that in youth, the mature prefrontal cortex, "the area of sober second thought," vital in considering enlistment, is among the last brain regions to mature and doesn't reach adult dimensions until the early 20s.[13]

But even growing numbers of children recognize that joining the occupation of Iraq is a must to avoid. Hence, the Pentagon has begun to turn to immigrants, dangling the prospect of citizenship before them as an inducement to enlist. Washington has instituted the Delayed Entry Program, which operates in high schools, GED programs and home-schooling networks and targets immigrants.[14] According to the stirring film, "The Short Life of Jose Antonio Gutierrez"—which details the experience of this man who was the first U.S. soldier to be killed during the invasion of March 2003 —he was one of approximately 32,000 so-called "green card soldiers" fighting in the ranks of the U.S. military.[15]

Increasingly desperate, it is becoming more and more evident that the Pentagon ultimately must turn to conscription—the draft—though it is recognized that this will only inflame antiwar sentiment. Soldiers and marines have been fighting in Afghanistan for six years, and Iraq for four, and the military is being stretched to the breaking point. It has begun to force injured soldiers back into combat before they have adequately recovered. Indeed, as put pithily by Lawrence Korb, Assistant Secretary of Defense during the Reagan Administration, the White House has placed itself in the tight-spot whereby they must either institute the draft—or "set a timetable to bring the troops home." [16]

Ironically, the wars in Iraq and Afghanistan are symptoms of a larger problem the Pentagon faces in seeking to replenish their ranks. The military is dominated by conservative hawks who exude a culture that many youth and minorities particularly find offensive and off-putting. This conservatism is dangerous for the nation; for example, in a 2004 poll the percentage of military respondents who characterized themselves as Republicans stood at 60%—though, fortunately, by the end of 2006 the number had plummeted to 46%. This latter trend is relatively new and no doubt reflects growing disquiet and unease with the debacle in Iraq, for as the columnist Rosa Brooks suggested, "between the end of the Vietnam War and the middle of the Clinton era, the U.S. military began to look like a wholly-owned subsidiary of the Republican Party." This was a "Republicanization of the military," which accompanied the "Republicanization of the American South." Tellingly, a "disproportionate number of military personnel are now stationed at bases in the South and Southwest." Given the rebellion in the military when the Clinton White House sought to liberalize regulations concerning gays in the ranks—which brought back memories of similar rebellions during the Kennedy White House, as encapsulated in the still stirring film about a military coup in the U.S., "Seven Days in May"—this apparent decline in GOP domination of the military must be welcomed. Indeed, a major reason one can be confident about the eventual end of the occupation is the growing rebellion in the military—against the policies of the Bush White House.[17]

This growing unrest among the brass congealed during the Spring of 2007. Outrage was expressed when Bush chose to veto the U.S. Troop Readiness, Veterans' Health and Iraq Accountability Act—which would have brought new benefits to those who serve and have served. That this move came from a man who is backed by those who demagogically claim to "Support the Troops" made this all the more maddening. The howling protest from various retired Generals reminded that it was a former General—and top aide to George H.W. Bush, i.e. Brent Scowcroft—who sought to spearhead opposition to the impending Iraqi invasion in the run-up to March 2003.[18]

But it would unwise to declare victory prematurely, for conservative hawks have created minefields of various sorts that will be exploding for years to come. The Southern Poverty Law Center, which has specialized in investigations of the racist right, has detected a disturbing trend that has infested the military. Aryan Nation graffiti has been seen in Baghdad—the latest bit of evidence suggesting that just as left-wing cadre often take root in factories, ultra-right cadre have come to find the U.S. military quite congenial. In 1996 following a decade-long rash of cases where extremists in the military were caught diverting huge arsenals of stolen firearms and explosives to neo-Nazi and white supremacist organizations, conducting guerilla training for paramilitary racist militias, and murdering "non-white" civilians, the Pentagon finally acted. One general ordered all 19,000 soldiers at Fort Lewis, Washington strip-searched in an attempt to find extremist tattoos.

Now it seems that with the decline in recruitment—or, perhaps, for other reasons—the Pentagon is turning a blind eye to the influx of neo-Nazis into their ranks.[19]

This disturbing development should be notably upsetting for U.S. imperialism's chief ally in the region, Israel, but this nation, which has become closely identified with conservative hawks in the U.S., is hardly in an advantageous position to object. Moreover, of late, critics of U.S. imperialism in the region have begun to look askance at Israel, which long has enjoyed an undeserved reputation as a vibrant "democracy" and feisty underdog. But then former U.S. President Jimmy Carter published a book excoriating Israel, suggesting in the process that "apartheid" was the term that best described their own occupation of the Palestinian territories. And as if that were not enough, two professors from Harvard and the University of Chicago—Stephen Walt and John Mearsheimer—published an essay, then a book,[20] averring that Israel was becoming a strategic liability for U.S. imperialism and only a potent domestic lobby on these shores barred an adequate ventilation of this situation. Predictably they were showered with a flood of invective, including charges of bigotry.

To be sure, the idea that the Israeli tail is wagging the dog of U.S. imperialism is not easy to swallow; likewise, it would be simplistic to ignore the influence that Saudi Arabia wields in Washington—not to mention Wall Street. Yes, U.S. imperialism sells billions of dollars of weapons to the Israeli colonialists—but sells a similar amount to the Saudi feudalists. A more comprehensive examination of Washington's policy in the region would have to conclude that the U.S. military-industrial complex benefits handsomely from the present standoff and would have much to lose if peace reigned. To that degree, the Israel Lobby in the U.S.—in the final analysis—is doing a dirty and dangerous job: for Washington.

Still, the Walt-Mearsheimer intervention is important not necessarily—as the lawyers might say—due to the truth of the matter asserted but, instead, what it suggests about the state of mind of the U.S. ruling class. For these elite professors have not been heretofore known as radical; indeed, they emerge from a field—academia—that has shown itself to be quite sly in cutting its conscience to fit the current fashions. In that sense, this book may be auguring a shift in U.S. policy in the region—or at least the beginning of a debate about one of the more pressing and outstanding issues to be resolved by the international community: the question of Palestinian statehood and rapid termination of the disastrous Israeli occupation. Telling in this regard is the lawsuit brought by law professor Erwin Chemerinsky, after the heroic U.S. national, Rachel Corrie, was mowed down by an Israeli-owned Caterpillar tractor after she tried to stop the destruction of Palestinian property. His suit against Caterpillar did not prevail, though shortly thereafter Prof. Chemerinsky was rejected on blatant political grounds in his bid to become the founding Dean of a new law school at the University of California-Irvine. Yet his detractors were compelled to retreat and he received the job in question, which was perceived—correctly—as a blow against the Israeli Lobby.[21]

Certainly Walt and Mearsheimer are at their strongest when they point to the Israeli lobby in seeking to shed light on U.S. imperialism's retrograde policy toward the Palestine Question, which—inter alia—has led to assaults on U.S. academics at Columbia University, De Paul University and other campuses who are deemed to be insufficiently backwards on this matter.

On the other hand, it should not be forgotten that Israel has been a valuable asset of U.S. imperialism in recent years, not least during the Cold War when it was essential to the propagation of the notion of the former Soviet Union as being a violator of human rights, via the campaign surrounding Soviet Jewry; emigration from the former USSR was helpful to Israel in meeting the demographic challenge of occupying the land in the face of high Arab birth rates. For years, U.S. imperialism has "prepositioned" vehicles, military equipment, even a 500-bed hospital in Israel for the use of U.S. Marines, Special Forces and Air Force fighter and bomber aircraft.[22]

U.S. imperialism may be even more dependent upon Israel since its other allies in the region are so unsteady. King Abdullah II of Jordan is beginning to resemble the late deposed Shah of Iran—a U.S. backed monarch, shaped by his powerful father, who surrounds himself with U.S. military hardware and spies. The consensus is that Jordanian intelligence—like the Shah's SAVAK—is a wholly owned subsidiary of the CIA and may be second only to British intelligence in collaborating with U.S. imperialism. This is occurring as a so-called "Islamic fundamentalist" movement continues to fester.[23]

Still, there is no doubt that a mutual souring of this once blazing hot romance is taking place. U.S. imperialism was displeased when during the Summer of 2006 Israel found itself bogged down in a conflict in Lebanon—principally with Hezbollah, perceived in Washington as an Iranian surrogate. This Israeli defeat seemingly lessened Israel's value in the eyes of U.S. imperialism, notably since it provided a guerilla template of instruction as to how to defeat the Zionist regime. As *Insight*, the magazine that caters to conservative hawks, put it, "the Israel failure...led to deep pessimism within the National Security Council and Pentagon...." Anthony Cordesman, a former Pentagon official now affiliated with the center-right Center for Strategic and International Studies, added, "the overall impression is that the Israeli government is not the kind of government that provides clear and effective management of war": there could be no greater liability for a small nation surrounded by real and imagined antagonists.[24] Similarly, U.S. imperialism has lost value in the eyes of Israel, given its inability to impose its will decisively on Iraq and the possible untoward consequences that flow from this epochal turning point.

Many in Washington are unhappy with Israel's "too smart by a half" approach to the Palestinians, which led to a concerted attempt to virtually create Hamas as a counterweight to Marxist influence within the Palestinian Liberation Organization. This was combined with Israel's stubbornness—ably assisted by their powerful lobby within the U.S.—in resisting the proclamation of Palestinian statehood. This has led to the rise of a Hamas regime that is proving itself to be similarly stubborn in accepting wholly the so-called "two state solution" and, of late, has routed the more secular Fatah party in Gaza. Not least for humanitarian reasons—and the fact that they were elected—the international community is gradually coming to the realization that Hamas must be engaged, despite their tepid embrace of the Oslo and Madrid peace processes. There are those in Washington who associate Hamas' rise with the concomitant ascension of the now reviled "Islamic fundamentalism"—and Israel is held not to be blameless.

Israel, on the other hand, feels that U.S. imperialism should be the last one to talk about seeking to manipulate ultra-nationalists in order to deflect the secular left, since Washington provided the playbook for this in Afghanistan and Socialist Yugoslavia. Moreover, for the longest, Washington has been open to collaboration with the Muslim Brotherhood—a godfather of Hamas. Al-Ikhwan al-Muslimun, as it is known in Arabic, is a sprawling and secretive society with followers in more than 70 nations. It is dedicated to creating an Islamic civilization that harks back to the caliphates of 1300 years ago, one that would segregate women from public life and scorn non-believers. For decades, the Brotherhood enjoyed the avid support of Riyadh, which assisted the group as it expanded into the U.S. itself, particularly in prisons where they found willing adherents among alienated African-Americans. In fact, in the U.S. the Brotherhood and its offshoots are virtually hegemonic, as they run hundreds of mosques and dozens of businesses engaging in profitable ventures, e.g. real estate and banking. The presumed architect of 9/11 told U.S. interrogators—who admittedly were using muscular techniques—that he was drawn to "violent jihad" after joining the Brotherhood in Kuwait at the age of 16. In Egypt, the Brotherhood wields wide influence—and the same can be said for Sudan, Algeria and a good deal of the region. Two former members of the Egyptian Brotherhood—Ayman Zawahiri (Bin Laden's version of Dick Cheney) and the so-called blind Sheik, Omar Abdel Rahman, who was convicted in 1995 of plotting to blow up New York landmarks—remain prominent. Another leader, known simply as "Nada," was jailed by G.A. Nasser (who Israel and U.S. imperialism schemed against relentlessly) but later became wealthy in Saudi Arabia and now lives in a sprawling villa in Italy. Now he is viewed by Washington as a financier of "terrorism" of Al Qaeda, Hamas, etc. Those familiar with revolutionary struggle have been struck by the Brotherhood's organization, which involves iron discipline and secrecy, cells and a covert military wing. They are deeply entrenched—and profoundly influential—in Saudi Arabia, which no doubt is relevant in explaining why U.S. imperialism seeks now to engage them. After all, the Saudi-Brotherhood connection was critical in the destabilization of Najibullah's Soviet-backed regime in Afghanistan and the birth of the Taliban. Bitter opposition to Israel is a key tenet for the Brotherhood, which is unsettling for the Zionist regime, particularly since some in Washington have come to view this grouping as a "moderate" force worthy of engagement.[25]

The toxicity of U.S. imperialism was no more disastrously revealed when fighting erupted between Hamas and Fatah in 2007. This was preceded by the arrival of hundreds of fighters in Gaza trained under U.S. auspices in neighboring nations[26] and a White House request for $83 billion in "non-lethal aid" to Fatah forces.[27] As the violence in Gaza was reaching an obstreperous crescendo, Alvaro De Soto, the well-respected

U.N. envoy of the so-called "Quartet" (the U.S., U.N., European Union and Russia), argued passionately that "the U.S. clearly pushed for a confrontation between Fatah and Hamas;" astoundingly, he cited a top-level U.S. official as asserting, "'I like this violence'." Just as astonishing was the fact that these mind-boggling words barely registered within the U.S. media. No better example can be cited to explain the growing hatred for U.S. imperialism in the region: similarly, this also suggests why Washington's failure to forthrightly address the Palestinian Question is a major factor in explicating the sharply declining prestige of U.S. imperialism generally.[28]

Increasingly nervous about the potency—and intentions—of U.S. imperialism, Israel has begun to hedge its bets, like other erstwhile allies of Washington: hence, the entente with a rising China. The Pentagon was stunned in the Summer of 2002 when Israeli-made anti-radar weapons were deployed with Chinese forces opposite Taiwan. This report emerged at the same time as a Chinese government technical journal asserted it is possible to defeat easily the Patriot anti-missile systems—one of U.S. imperialism's proudest creations. Washington quickly concluded that Beijing's detailed dissection of this system indicated that it had possession of it—which was supposedly covertly supplied by Israel. The Patriot had been deployed in Israel by the Pentagon during the 1991 Gulf War. Then Israel was accused by the Pentagon of sharing restricted U.S. weapons technology with China related to a battlefield laser gun. Allegedly U.S. contractors working in Israel espied Chinese technicians working with one of the Israeli companies involved in the laser program. The *Washington Times*, read more religiously by conservative hawks than the Holy Bible, was not pleased by these developments.[29]

But it will not be easy for Israel to deploy China as a counterweight to U.S. imperialism—even if Beijing wanted to play this role, which is quite doubtful. For Beijing has its own interests in the region, access to oil being among them, and here closeness to Israel is perceived broadly as a liability, something to which Washington can well attest. Thus, it was not overly surprising when in the Spring of 2006 Israel issued an unusually strong rebuke of China over its decision to invite a senior Hamas minister to attend a Sino-Arab conference in Beijing. Earlier Israel was displeased when Russia, then Sweden made similar overtures to Hamas.[30]

Thus, Israeli colonialism and U.S. imperialism may be fated—or doomed—to be aligned, for their interests dovetail broadly, even though there will be hiccups. The question on the horizon is whether the Walt-Mearsheimer book is an indication that this hiccup can become a deadly epileptic convulsion. This is unlikely in the short term, but the future is unclear. For example, after the London poodle, Tony Blair, was forced to step down as Prime Minister in 2007, it was U.S. imperialism and Israel that maneuvered to provide him with the post of Middle East envoy, succeeding former World Bank President James Wolfensohn. This appointment was badly received in Brussels, casting doubt on the rumors about Blair eventually becoming "President" of the European Union. Wolfensohn had quit after Israel failed to honor a U.S.- brokered agreement that would have opened Gaza to greater economic opportunities and ties with the West Bank. Wolfensohn was not opposed to engagement with Hamas—anathema to Israel and U.S. imperialism, thus far: although it is apparent that if Washington engages the Muslim Brotherhood, as it seeks to do, then ultimately it will do the same with its offspring, Hamas. The larger point is, however, that the Blair appointment was a typical move by the Israeli colonialists and the U.S. imperialists—greeted with either yelps or yawns in the international community;[31] but it is doubtful if the declining prestige of Washington and its equally declining financial fortunes as reflected in the descending dollar, will allow such unilateralism to take place as this century unwinds. And at that point it is easy to imagine that a diminished Israel will seek to solidify further its relations with China—to the consternation of U.S. imperialism.

Part of the glue that bonds Israel and the U.S. is the mutual antipathies they share—once this embraced the former Soviet Union and today is focused on Iran and Syria. Though conservative hawks see isolating Damascus as an article of faith, in the long term it may be easier for U.S. imperialism to engage with this regime than it will be for Israel, which must return the Golan Heights in order to resume normal relations with Syria.[32] Iran may be different, however. This is something of a turnabout. As Trita Parsi observes in his new book,[33] despite the rather vitriolic denunciations of Israel—and questioning of the Holocaust—that have emerged from Teheran, Iran continues to have one of the largest Jewish populations in the region outside of Israel itself. Recall that the scandalous Iran-Contra episode of the Reagan Administration involved direct collaboration between and among U.S. imperialism, Israel and Iran.

Still, it would be imprudent to ignore the war whoops being emitted in Washington—principally from the conservative hawks who engineered the Iraqi debacle—designed to destabilize and intimidate Iran. Rumors now being floated suggest that U.S. imperialism will attack Iran militarily at some point before the end of the calamitous Bush regime in early 2009—and those fanning the flames include some of Israel's most important supporters in the U.S, including the writer Norman Podhoretz who is calling for "World War IV" (World War III, in case you missed it, was the Cold War) and Senator Joseph Lieberman of Connecticut. Uniting against Iraq may be a way by which Israel and the U.S. can paper over their own troubles. Now the bellicose language from the Oval Office may very well be empty verbiage, tailored to compel Teheran to give up out of fear what cannot be obtained at the negotiating table. Yet the fact remains that the hapless Bush team has placed 160,000 U.S. sitting ducks right next door to Iran who easily could be victimized in the wake of the predicted bombing assault on Iranian nuclear facilities—the ostensible bone of contention.

Yet M. Javad Zarif, Iran's Ambassador to the United Nations, had a point when he wondered why the U.N. Security Council was forced to convene on the Saturday before Christmas 2006 to vote on Resolution 1737—against Iran's nuclear program. Where was the urgency? Iran had not attacked any UN member state. In fact, said the Ambassador, Iran has not waged an offensive war in two centuries. Iran was not on the verge of building a nuclear weapon. To the contrary, as a study released in late 2006 by the National Academy of Sciences concluded, Iran needs nuclear energy despite its oil and gas reserves.

At the same time Iran has categorically rejected the development, stockpiling and use of nuclear weapons on both ideological and strategic grounds. It has remained committed to the Nuclear Nonproliferation Treaty—which it ratified in 1970—and has been prepared to provide guarantees that it would never withdraw from the treaty. (Contrast the U.S. and Israel in this regard: both are nuclear powers, with the U.S. being the only nation ever to use this monster weapon.)

All of Iran's nuclear facilities have been inspected by the International Atomic Energy Agency. Iran has stated its readiness to place them under an even more stringent regime, as it did from December 2003 to February 2006, when more than 2000 person-days of scrutiny resulted in repeated statements by the IAEA that there was no existence of a weapons program. There is no actual evidence that Iran is trying to build a nuclear weapon and that even if it so desired, it would not be capable of developing one before 2010 or 2015. (And the entire non-nuclear proliferation regime turns on a major point that has been studiously ignored— that the existing nuclear weapons would move decisively toward a non-nuclear weapon world: instead the U.S. in particular has moved in an opposing direction.)

In March 2005 Iran offered a comprehensive and far-reaching package to the so-called EU3—Britain, France and Germany—including national legislation to permanently ban developing or using nuclear weapons, technical guarantees against proliferation and unprecedented, around-the-clock IAEA inspections. Due to Washington's objections— and despite their own initial enthusiasm—the EU3 refused to engage in negotiations. This was one of many initiatives by Teheran to negotiate this matter—but U.S. imperialism and Israel have decided to stonewall.[34]

One of the chief slogans of former Pentagon chief, Donald Rumsfeld, has been that if one has a problem, the way to deal with it is to expand it. Even the EU3, often willing to bend to the will of Washington, is now pushing back. In August 2007 these nations, joined by others, descended on Capitol Hill and in an extraordinary maneuver befitting the profundity of the crisis, stepped up a lobbying campaign against moves that would mandate sanctions on energy companies that invested more than $20 million in Iran. This law would be devastating to Total of France and Royal Dutch Shell in particular. Along with Repsol of Spain they are involved in a project worth up to $10 billion to produce Iran's first lique-fied natural gas. This law would have the not coincidental effect of ham-stringing the chief rivals of Exxon-Mobil.[35] The thrust of this new legisla-tion is to strengthen the existent Iran Sanctions Act of 1996.

Interestingly, as the Jewish-American weekly *Forward* pointed out on 27 May 2007, generally the Republicans have been more hawkish on Iran than their Democrat counterparts, with the latter more willing to absorb the painful and expensive lessons of Iraq.

This legislation is merely the tip of a statutory spear that is being launched by state and municipal bodies nationally, demanding divestment from any companies that have holdings in Iran. The Israel Lobby—notably the notorious American Israel Public Affairs Committee—has been in the vanguard of this crusade. New York pension funds alone own nearly $1 billion of stock in three Fortune 500 companies tied to Iran. In 2006 Missouri took the lead in this realm, but it is being followed by Ohio, Pennsylvania and California.[36] On the question of sanctions against Iran, Democrats and Republicans have joined hands.[37]

One thing is clear: this crisis is about energy—not nuclear, but the staple of the Lone Star state: oil. Iran is the world's fourth largest produc-er of oil and has a strategic location abreast the Strait of Hormuz, through which 20% of the world's production passes. Today Iran supplies China with 4% of its oil; France with 7%; South Korea with 9%; Japan with 10%; Italy with 11%; Belgium with 14%; Turkey with 22% and Greece with 24%. Germany is Iran's largest trade partner though it will soon be replaced by China, whose role in Teheran is growing exponentially. A mil-itary attack against Iran by U.S. imperialism would hamper its chief com-petitors, as it provided Washington with a larger say in the all-important petroleum market.[38]

Whatever doubt existed about the importance of oil to U.S. imperi-alism's maneuvers in the Persian Gulf have been removed of late. First, there was the shameful display in April 2003, when U.S. troops stood by idly as museums and archives and the nation's patrimony was looted—

while it guarded the Oil Ministry as if it were Fort Knox (which it was, in a sense). Since then, Iraqi Communists and trade unionists have been full-throated in their denunciations of blatant attempts by the imperialists to steal the nation's oil.

A strike by Iraqi oil workers in June 2007 brought this issue to the fore. The Iraqi Federation of Oil Unions shut down the pipelines from the Rumeila fields near Basra, in the south, to the Baghdad refinery and the rest of the nation. Walking in the footsteps of Iraq's heroic unions of yore, the oil workers has thousands of members. (The electrical workers' union is the first national union to be led by a woman, Hashmeya Muhsin Hussein.) One of the "benchmarks" that Baghdad is being compelled to meet would facilitate foreign takeover of their most precious resource: petroleum. Bending to pressure, Prime Minister Nouri al-Maliki respond-ed by calling units of the 10th Division of the Iraqi army and surrounding the strikers at Sheiba, near Basra. Arrest warrants for strike leaders were issued. Then the Prime Minister folded, agreeing to the union's demand to slow down implementation of the oil law.[39]

This was the latest heroic action by the oil workers who—along with spreading dissidence within the U.S. military itself—stand as a major obstacle to the implementation of the draconian plans of U.S. imperialism. John Sweeney, top U.S. labor leader, has spoken admiringly of how the union has braved "raids" on their offices, "seizure of union records, destruction of union office equipment, freezing union bank accounts, arrest, beating and kidnapping of union activists and even assassination of union leaders." He backed the oil workers' effort to block privatization.[40]

This was not greeted with glee in Washington. Recall that the much-heralded "Iraq Study Group" led by former Secretary of State, James A. Baker III and former congressman, Lee Hamilton, proposed the rapid pri-vatization of Iraq's oil coupled with a quick infusion of foreign invest-ment. There is a bipartisan consensus in Washington that transcends party differences that privatization should be avidly pursued.

The response from Washington? If Baghdad fails to pursue privati-zation, then Washington provides no reconstruction funds to a war-rav-aged nation. Though official Washington views privatization to be as appealing as parenthood, actually no other nation in the region has done so—including Saudi Arabia, Kuwait, Bahrain and Iran. But Exxon-Mobil now perceives that it will have increasing difficulty competing with pub-lic sector oil firms as this century proceeds, so forcing Iraq to privatize its oil is seen as a useful precedent that can be used to intimidate those who, so far, refuse to take this path.

And if these nations do not comply with Washington's—and Exxon Mobil's—demand for privatization, then the bases that U.S. imperialism is building in Iraq may come in handy. It was on 19 April 2003 that alert readers of *The New York Times* noticed the headline that encapsulated a key reason for the then ongoing invasion: "Pentagon Expects Long-Term Access to Four Key Bases in Iraq." This report was not imaginary. Thus, decades after the end of the Pacific War, the Pentagon continues to control 20% of the Japanese island of Okinawa, which is part of 725 military bases in 38 nations featuring 255,000 military personnel that U.S. imperialism administers.[41]

And in case the mailed fist of armed violence proves insufficient—as it has thus far in Iraq—the old tactic of spurring ethnic division can be trotted out. That was the import of the revelation that the Hunt Oil Company of Dallas, Texas, led by Ray L. Hunt, a close friend of George W. Bush, (and a member of the Foreign Intelligence Advisory Board), had inked a deal with the provincial government in Kurdistan, Iraq. In defiance of the central government in Baghdad, this government passed its own oil deal. No doubt playing upon the tensions between Kurds and non-Kurdish Iraqis will prove useful in insuring that the deal with Hunt Oil is honored.

So it comes to this: massive bloodletting and fragmented lives just so Bush's oil cronies can corner the market on oil. One had thought that this kind of brigandage had expired in previous centuries. Yet such brazen adventurism cannot halt the inevitable devolution of U.S. imperialism—least of all can this trend be arrested on the continent that is the most populous and, if present trends continue, will continue to be the global pacesetter economically: Asia.

3: China's Peaceful Rise/U.S. Imperialism's Inexorable Decline

William Safire was not happy.

This conservative hawk and *New York Times* columnist was in conversation with his former boss, the late Richard M. Nixon, and the sly and devious former President was not exactly ecstatic either. What had disconcerted these two ideologues?

"Before Nixon died," recalled Safire later, "I asked him—on the record—if perhaps we had gone a bit overboard on selling the American public on the political benefits of increased trade with China. That old realist," continued Safire, "who had played the China card to exploit the split in the Communist world, replied with some sadness, that he was not as hopeful as he had once been: 'We may have created a Frankenstein [monster],'" lamented the otherwise hard-boiled anticommunist.[1]

Nixon was on to something. For the chattering classes have yet to detect that the former Soviet Union collapsed not least due to the encirclement of it—and resultant military pressure—in which China played an essential role, notably after Nixon's epochal trip to Beijing some thirty-five odd years ago. This led directly to China waging war on Socialist Vietnam, aiding genocide in Cambodia (then Kampuchea), collaborating with U.S. imperialism in Southern Africa and Afghanistan, and forcing an overstretch of Moscow's resources, which led directly to the 1989-1991 crisis.

Yet once again history has proven to be a cruel taskmaster for because of Nixon's decision to "exploit the split in the Communist world," U.S. imperialism just exchanged one Communist antagonist in Moscow for a larger, far stronger Communist antagonist in Beijing—and this is a victory? No wonder this strategic foul-up is hardly discussed in this nation. But reality has a way of intruding irrespective of whether one perceives it, and the fact is that China is on a glide path to become the leading economic—and possibly military—power on this planet at some point in the very near future. Ironically, a nation which had etched white supremacy, then anticommunism on its escutcheon, will be surpassed by a nation led by the Communist Party of China—and will bear no small responsibility for this precedent-shattering development.

This has to rank as the chief irony of the era, not unlike Paris out-smarting itself when it supported rebels against British rule in North America, or Britain appointing Japan as its watchdog in Asia at the beginning of the 20th century—then being bitten viciously in December 1941. Yet it is unavoidable that Nixon's trip opened the door to a flood of foreign direct investment to China—particularly from the U.S. itself—which has created a manufacturing juggernaut and financial titan.

To be fair, bourgeois analysts have not exactly ignored this phenomenon. Joshua Cooper Ramo, Ted Fishman and James Kynge of the *Financial Times* are among the writers who have peered into their crystal balls and walked away wondrously with visions of China percolating in their brains.

How could they not? The question that no doubt will animate future historians is why so few linked the rise of China to the previous strategic imperative—bolstering Beijing to better confront Moscow. It is as if U.S. elites find it too painful to contemplate that what they deem to be their major victory—the Soviet Union's collapse—is intimately connected to what may be an insurmountable challenge: the peaceful rise of China.

Actually, one does not have to wait until the future to get a grip on China's weight in the international community. As the *Los Angeles Times* put it, "China's reach now extends from the Australian desert through the Sahara to the Amazonian jungle—and it's those regions supplying goods for China, not just the other way around. China has stepped up its political and diplomatic presence, most notably in Africa, where it is funneling billions of dollars in aid. And it is increasingly shaping the lifestyle of people around the world, as the United States did before it, right down to the Mandarin language courses being taught in schools from Argentina to Virginia." For if China's growth continues at present levels, its consumer market will be world's largest by 2015. The Chinese already eat 32% of the world's rice, build with 47% of its cement and smoke one of every three cigarettes. China is buying coal mining equipment from Poland and drilling for oil and gas in Ethiopia and Nigeria. It has invested hundreds of millions of dollars into Zambia's copper industry. It is the world's biggest market for mobile phones, headed for 520 million handsets this year. I recall when I spent a year in Hong Kong, the Special Administrative Region of China, beginning in 1999 and noticed that the women who emptied my waste basket at Hong Kong University all had mobile phones—which was not true of a good deal of the expatriate faculty: including myself.[2]

What is angering conservative hawks is Beijing's reluctance to sign on to every ruinous ruse devised by Washington. Thus, Beijing—in the face of adamant opposition from U.S. imperialism—has greatly strengthened its relations with Teheran, signing since 2004 several long-term energy exploration production and delivery contracts with Iran worth more than $100 billion. In 2006 China invested in Iran's domestic oil-refining industry, agreeing to expand the country's gasoline output significantly — investments that, to Washington's dismay, will greatly undermine economic sanctions on Teheran that target Iran's fuel imports. In early 2006 Iran successfully test-fired two new, sophisticated cruise missiles that were developed with Beijing's assistance.

China and North Korea have long been close allies — as any student of the disastrous war of U.S. imperialism against this latter nation may recall. Beijing has stood in the way of U.N sanctions against Pyongyang. China has invested substantially in the development of Syria's transportation infrastructure, as well as in energy exploration and production. China is also a key military supplier to Syria. Hugo Chavez of Venezuela has visited China four times since 1999 and China has become a major investor in Caracas' energy sector and its infrastructure, including railroads, ports and crude-oil tankers, not to mention telecom, mining and agricultural sectors. In turn, Caracas is shifting its oil exports toward China.[3]

By 2020, China is slated to become the world's leading automaker.[4] According to Credit Suisse First Boston, the powerful investment bank, "in 10 years, China will be the world's largest producer of information technology hardware." [5] China is moving up the industrial food chain, poised to take the world lead in the production of Internet Appliances, the "next big thing" after the personal computer and the mobile telephone.[6] Chrysler recently signed a deal with China's biggest automaker, Chery, to produce cars for export to the U.S. and elsewhere, in the first attempt by a U.S. automaker to use China as a manufacturing base for world markets.[7]

Only recently top U.S. steel executives demanded action to stem the flood of Chinese steel coming to this nation. By 2006 China's exports of finished steel products to the U.S. reached 5.5 million tons, up more than 130% from the previous year, becoming the third-largest exporter of steel to the U.S. after the European Union and Canada.[8] U.S. manufacturers appreciative of cheap Chinese steel were not necessarily on board with this demand. One of the problems that the U.S. ruling elite faces is that it will not be easy to knock together unanimity to confront China among its members, given the massive U.S. corporate investments in that nation.

Nonetheless, it would be foolish to think that a trade conflict with China could not morph easily into a militarized conflict. Beijing was stunned and angered in 2007 when the U.S. Commerce Department slapped anti-subsidy duties on imports of glossy paper from China. This was the first time countervailing duties against China had been brought since 1991, when the Commerce Department rejected two similar requests.[9] But as *Business Week* noted in the back story to this bewildering bit of news, behind this tariff was Cerberus Capital—recent purchaser of Chrysler—which also controls New-Page Corporation, which also produces glossy paper. Cerberus' chairman is John Snow, U.S. Treasury Secretary from 2003-2006. This mouthpiece of state monopoly capital felt compelled to ask, should the U.S. "start a trade war with China to protect private equity investors?" As long as the left is omitted from the conversation, the answer will be yes—and, further, that this trade war could easily devolve into another kind of conflict.[10]

The North Atlantic powers are finding it increasingly difficult to compete with China, which forces them deeper into hypocrisy as they contradict their usual "free market" rhetoric by imposing tariffs and busily constructing protectionist walls. The latest evidence is the charge from the European Investment Bank that it has lost business to Chinese banks because they apply lower ethical and environmental standards.[11] Boeing and Europe's Airbus stopped squabbling for business long enough to unite in hostility to China's plan to mount a challenge to their dominance in the global market for big passenger jets by setting up a state-owned company to build the aircraft. In the U.S. it was unclear what agitated more: [12] China's challenge or the decision to bolster their already formidable public sector. Moreover, just as common opposition to Iran has helped U.S. imperialism and Israel to paper over their sharp differences, joint hostility to China's rise led the reliably conservative *Wall Street Journal* to detect a "unified stance" on Beijing, particularly concerning trade and its supposed "defense buildup." [13]

Typically, U.S. imperialism, instead of looking homeward to ascertain why the self-proclaimed "sole remaining superpower" and "indispensable nation" is now grappling with cascading problems—a falling dollar, signs of a financial meltdown, a draining quagmire in Iraq—instead has looked for blame across the Pacific. In a bi-partisan maneuver, the South Carolina Republican Senator, Lindsay Graham, and the New York Democrat, Charles Schumer, have united to demand that China revalue its currency upward on the premise that it is a culprit in explicating the startling trade deficit with the U.S. that is in Beijing's favor. But *Business Day* of South Africa is not alone in pointing out that even if China were to comply, this would hardly solve the problem. In fact, it was asserted, if the dollar and the yuan traded freely, the former would "fall drastically"— which would increase imports dramatically, including automobiles, toys, computers and the like. Besides, China could then curb its purchases of U.S. Treasury bills, which could force the U.S. to raise taxes—or slash programs sharply, including education and health care.[14] As an analyst in the *Asia Times* put it, "between 70% and 80% ($700 billion to $800 billion) of China's foreign exchange reserves consist of U.S. dollar denominated assets such as U.S. Treasury securities. With such large dollar assets, it is ridiculous to believe that Beijing will undertake any large revaluation of the yuan against the dollar. A 25% revaluation of the yuan against the greenback would reduce the value of China's foreign assets by $175-$200 billion." China could slowly but steadily and systematically begin to dump its dollar assets — which could be happening as I write.[15]

Suggestive of the growing tension, China's Vice-Premier, Wu Yi, traveled to Washington in the Spring of 2007 to issue a sharp warning to the U.S. to stop pressuring China to engage in "economic reform" — shorthand for further privatizing of the public sector and opening up the economy to further plunder by U.S. imperialism: this would be tantamount to China pressuring the U.S. to bolster its careworn public sector.[16]

Strategically, what U.S. imperialism needs to extend its lease on hegemony is a major power to do what Beijing did to Moscow during the Cold War era. The most likely choice is India. Recently the investment banking firm, Goldman Sachs of Wall Street, whose executives as a matter of course seem to have a lock on being Secretary of the Treasury, predicted that India "would...overtake the U.S. to become the largest economy in the world after China by 2042."[17] Other oracles forecast this occurring much sooner. The problem is that the Asian giant that is India has not one but two influential Communist Parties, both of which are adamantly opposed to seeing their homeland being manipulated by unscrupulous U.S. imperialists. Still, Washington has not stopped trying, and the late summer of 2007 witnessed a lineup engaged in military maneuvers not far from China's borders, a lineup that U.S. imperialism envisions as a kind of Asian NATO — i.e. India, Japan, Australia and Singapore.[18]

But recreating NATO in Asia will not be simple. Though tensions lingering from the Pacific War continue to plague relations between Tokyo and Beijing, pacifist and anti-militarist sentiment may run deeper in Japan than any other major nation. Australia, with a population barely topping 20 million, does not have enough heft to matter globally and, in any case, has a Labour Party poised to seize and retain power with pervasive anti-imperialist sentiments (generated in no small part by revulsion at the disastrous U.S. occupation of Iraq), led by a Sino-phile, Kevin Rudd, whose mastery of the Chinese language surpasses fluency. Opportunistic Singapore, which has a Chinese majority, will "go with the flow" — as evidenced by the fact that their pre-eminent leader, Lee Kuan Yew, collaborated with Japan during the Pacific War.

Then there is another factor that will hamper U.S. imperialism's ability to forge an anti-China bloc. During the conflict with the then Soviet

Union, much ado was made about the alleged plight of artists and intellectuals, and a number of them defected to these shores where they could be integrated into leading circles. However, the white supremacy that facilitated this trend vis-à-vis Russia may not operate as smoothly concerning Asia. Of late New Delhi has been abuzz about the case of Neelima Tirumalasetti, of Indian origin, who has filed suit in Texas against a U.S. firm. This information technology analyst was subjected allegedly to repeated racial harassment and discrimination after the company for which she worked in Texas decided to outsource work to India. Stories about her did not fail to note that Indian nationals are developing a rather low opinion of the U.S., since call centers started opening in their country which has led employees to being assaulted with abusive and racial outpourings from North American callers. In early 2005 IBM added more than 14,000 jobs in India after slashing 13,000 posts in Europe and the U.S. and, apparently, this contributed to the harassment of the beleaguered Ms. Tirumalasetti. Prior to her travails, India-born PepsiCo President, Indra Nooyi, a powerful corporate leader, was assailed when she asserted—quite accurately—at Columbia Business School in Manhattan, that the U.S. was the "middle finger" of the world, not least due to its imperialist foreign policy. She was then subjected to a barrage of intensely personal racist and sexist insult. India, a quite proud nation was not happy to see a favorite daughter treated so shabbily.[19] Washington's close cousin in London also has been criticized by New Delhi: the government itself objected to abuse hurled by celebrity Jade Goody at Indian actress Shilpa Shetty on a British "reality" television show. The suspicion of more than latent racism stirred old memories about the white supremacist colonial project foisted on India for centuries and further compromised the ability of the Anglo-American power to disguise its old aims in the finery of the new.[20]

One of the many defects of imperialism is how it breeds national chauvinism, and given this nation's troubled history of anti-African bias, the U.S. has a particular difficulty with this problem. So when a Hollywood blockbuster on the bombing of Pearl Harbor by Japan was about to premier a few years ago there was a general unease among Asian-Americans, some of whom fought shoulder to shoulder with the U.S. military during this conflict. But as one commentator told *The New York Times*, "I think it [the movie] is going to create a lot of animosity, not only against the Japanese but anyone who has an Asian face." [21]

In short, because of white supremacy, it will be not as easy to convince "anyone with an Asian face"—notably those of Japan and India, not to mention China[22]—about the benign intentions of U.S. imperialism, compared to the previous experience with nationals of the former Soviet

Union.

Washington's bet on pitting Japan against China, propelled by Tokyo's depredations e.g. in Nanking in the late 1930s, may be misplaced; for example, France and Germany were at war repeatedly in the late 19th century and the first few decades in the 20th century—then they became the joint anchor of the emerging European Union. Who is to say this will not be duplicated in Asia—particularly since Japan has an increasingly influential Communist Party, some of whose members played a pivotal role in the monumental liberation of China in 1949?

Noteworthy in that regard was what was described as an "unusual consensus" between Tokyo and Beijing in support of an Asian currency unit. As a senior Chinese economist put it, this would "reduce their reliance on a weakening dollar." It also seemed that this stunning development had other motives. First of all, the euro—the common currency of the European Union—had demonstrated the advantages of such financial integration. And perhaps more important, reducing reliance on a weakening dollar, could compel the U.S. to do something about its yawning deficit and massive trade imbalances—besides forcing the rest of the world to provide low interest loans.[23] Historically, U.S. imperialism has resisted stoutly efforts at Asian integration. Recall that the Clinton Administration in the aftermath of the 1997 currency crisis quashed efforts by Japan and Malaysia to establish an Asian Monetary Fund. Yet in June 2006, as further evidence of the weakening of U.S. imperialism, Washington acquiesced to the idea of an ACU, though it could ultimately present mortal danger for the dollar—akin to the euro.[24] Similarly worthy of note was the recommendation from the influential Washington economist, Fred Bergsten, who suggested that China should dump its gigantic dollar holdings—in favor of the yen, which is as undervalued as the dollar is overvalued.[25]

Certainly this would make sense from a geo-political sense in that it would serve to neutralize Tokyo as it sent a shot over the bow of the U.S. It would complement the rapid expansion of Sino-Japanese trade. In an important milestone in 2004, Japanese trade with China reached $168 billion, allowing China to replace the United States as Japan's largest trading partner for the first time since World War II. There are at least a million Chinese workers directly employed by Japanese companies in China and another 9.2 million employed by Japanese sub-contractors.[26]

In the 1980s there was mordant hysteria about Japan in certain elite circles in the U.S. View the Hollywood movie "Iron Maze" for example, produced in 1991, to get a glimpse of the escalating concern. U.S. auto manufacturers have not purged themselves of such feelings as of today but the rapid rise of China and the need for Japan to serve as a counterweight makes expression of these sentiments problematic at best. For the market share of Toyota, Nissan and Honda in the U.S. continues its steady ascension, while Ford, GM and Chrysler are shedding load—in early 2006 Ford announced that it would be closing 14 plants in North America, as its credit rating was downgraded to junk status. Like China, Japan enjoys a huge trade surplus with the U.S.. Meanwhile, the U.S. car-makers are weighted down with health care costs while their competitor in Japan has the benefit of a nationalized health care system borne by the public sector. The point is that despite the urge to blame Japan demagogically for Detroit's problems, as was done so notoriously in the 1980s—which led to the slaying of a Chinese-American, Vincent Chin, in a spate of anti-Asian violence—this has not occurred to the same extent today, not least due to the desire to maintain good relations with Tokyo in order to counter China more effectively.[27]

Still, as the crisis of U.S. imperialism deepens and popular discourse hinders the ability to point the finger of accusation where it belongs—in the direction of the ruling class—the impulse to find external scapegoats, particularly those who cannot be defined as "white," is simply too tempting to ignore. Thus it was in early 2007 that a number of powerful Democratic Party politicos turned their spotlight of indictment temporarily away from Beijing and turned toward Tokyo. Japan, it was said, is deliberately keeping its currency weak to encourage exports—but this accusation could hardly take flight in light of Tokyo's designation as a critical outpost of the anti-China strategy.[28] Consider that one of the many advantages that Japan has over the U.S. is that—unlike Washington—Tokyo has to listen to powerful Communist and Social Democratic parties, which means that national decisions are more rational and realistic compared to Washington, where center-right ideological hegemony is a virtual biblical injunction. Hence, Washington was stunned in the Spring of 2001 when Japan's Foreign Minister stated the obvious (one definition of a political gaffe is when a politician stumbles and states what is obvious to any sentient being). Makiko Tanaka said that the White House's lunatic scheme of anti-missile defense—Son of Star Wars—"may be influenced by support groups (for Bush) such as the petroleum industry in his constituency of Texas." [29] Official Washington was stunned and appalled when recently retired top U.S. banker, Alan Greenspan said as much, acknowledging the primacy of oil interests in shaping imperialist foreign policy, especially the invasion and occupation of Iraq.[30]

Though Japan remains under military occupation by U.S. imperialism, it remains the world's second largest economy, the second largest contributor to the United Nations, the International Monetary Fund, the World Bank, the Asian Development Bank—and just about every other multilateral institution extant. China's rise notwithstanding, two-thirds of Asian GDP is Japanese, and Japan's economy is seven times the size of China's. Yet the strategic point is that if Tokyo does not join enthusiastically in the latest anticommunist crusade—which at the moment seems doubtful—it is questionable if it can gain momentum.

Another Asian giant that may turn a cold shoulder to the conservative hawks is Indonesia. Being the world's largest predominantly Muslim nation, Indonesia will have a hard time convincing its populace why it should join a nation, the U.S., that is so reviled by those of the Islamic faith because of its bloody wars in Iraq and Afghanistan, with Iran now being stared at through the periscope. Moreover, Jakarta remains peeved that during the height of the Asian financial crisis of 1997, it was the "Washington Consensus" imposed by the IMF that plunged the nation into deeper woe. The palm-oil, timber and mining businesses, all invested in heavily by U.S.-based businesses, have been particularly harmful to the Indonesian environment and often to the indigenous people whose lands they use. Washington placed enormous pressure on Jakarta to make sure that U.S. investors harmed in the aftermath of the 1997 crisis were compensated—which did not win many friends in Indonesia.[31] Many Indonesians have not forgotten Washington's lengthy backing of the now discredited Suharto dictatorship, nor the human rights violations committed by his military in East Timor. On the other hand, there is resentment of China stemming from many factors, e.g. its influence on the Communist Party there, which may have contributed to the catastrophic 1965 coup that brought Suharto to power—and led to the death of 500,000 or more. Plus, one key to China's spectacular growth in recent years is the substantial support it has received from the Chinese bourgeoisie in Southeast Asia, who—like dominant elites elsewhere –are not exactly popular, least of all in Indonesia, as the Yale scholar Amy Chua pointed out cogently.[32] However, China's diplomatic and economic offensive in Indonesia has gone a long way to smoothing ruffled feathers in Jakarta.[33]

One of the disadvantages that U.S. imperialism will face in Southeast Asia, however, is the fact that it has established itself as the new homeland for retrograde refugees globally. Consider how certain Cuban-Americans in South Florida have poisoned relations with Havana. Today U.S. imperialism is desperately interested in improving relations with Socialist Vietnam so it could better turn it against China—just as the latter attacked this besieged Southeast Asian nation after it had barely recovered from a near genocidal pummeling at the hands of Washington. Among the many roadblocks to this nasty anti-China scheme—beyond the farsightedness of Hanoi's ruling Communist Party—is a segment of the Vietnamese-American community headquartered in Orange County,

California. Their "never-say-die" attitude, clamoring for the impossible—overthrowing Communist rule in their former homeland—is an irritant complicating imperialist maneuvers. Similarly, many Laotian-Americans were aghast when it was revealed that a former National Guard lieutenant colonel and Hmong leaders met in March 2007 with California Highway Patrol officials to try to get law enforcement training for participants in a plot to overthrow the Laotian government. Vang Pao—now resident in Orange County—led CIA-backed forces in Laos during the war against Vietnam, then became a leader among Hmong refugees who later settled in the U.S. His plan was to use CHP training to develop a cadre of officers to help with the military operations and provide security in the "new" regime. He was assisted by retired U.S. Lieutenant Colonel Harrison Ulrich Jack, a West Point graduate, known to have good connections at the highest level in Washington.[34] Official Washington feigned ignorance, though governments in the region took note.

The Korean peninsula—where 37,000 U.S. troops are stationed, a half-century after a truce was proclaimed after Washington's aggression—is yet another flashpoint. North Korea was designated as part of the "axis of evil," along with Iraq and Iran, yet it has not faced as much belligerence as its other two "partners," principally because Seoul and Beijing refuse to capitulate. As for Pyongyang, in 1994 it signed the Agreed Framework with the U.S., defusing the ostensible basis for tensions, i.e. the North's development of nuclear technology. The deal was that the U.S. would aid the Democratic Peoples Republic of Korea—the North—in acquiring modern, light-water nuclear reactors that would produce nuclear energy but not weapons and move toward normal relations. But the arrogant Bush team reneged on this deal—before sheepishly being compelled to accept its broad outline.[35]

U.S. imperialism has had difficulty in finding Quislings in Seoul, as evidenced by the extraordinary public dressing down South Korea's leader administered to Bush during a bilateral meeting in Sydney, Australia in September 2007.[36] South Koreans have hardly forgotten the terror inflicted by U.S. imperialism during the war, particularly at No Gun Ri in July 1950, which in the mind of Seoul has taken on the same depth and emotional intensity that My Lai invokes in Vietnam.[37] Seoul and its chaebols—or powerful business interests—have invested heavily in China and are hardly interested in jeopardizing their massive investments by going on a fool's errand devised by conservative hawks in Washington.

China's relations with India have improved since Beijing's unfortunate war with New Delhi in 1962—though it would be foolish to ignore the complaint of former Indian Defense Minister George Fernandes that India's biggest rival in coming decades would be China.[38] Nevertheless, repeated high-level visits have led to the reopening of the snowy Himalaya pass, a lonely road linking Asia's two giants, this after a four decade-long diplomatic roadblock.[39] Thus, *China Daily* seemed pleased to report in late 2005 that "India and China, often fierce rivals in the race for global energy supplies, have won a joint bid to buy Petro-Canada's 37 percent stake in Syrian oil fields for 573 million dollars....this is the first time the two Asian giants have bid together for overseas reserves to feed their economies." It could have been added that this was a further blow to Exxon-Mobil and other U.S. corporations who, once more, were flummoxed by a state-owned oil company, this time New Delhi's, which took the lead in these negotiations.[40]

Because U.S. imperialism seeks to woo India, it had to be reserved in response. This underscores what is unfolding in the world: just as U.S. imperialism had to build up China in return for confronting the former Soviet Union, now Washington has to build up India in hopes of enlisting New Delhi in a confrontation with Beijing. It does not require a seer to foresee that the end result of this process will be a diminished U.S. imperialism—and a rising India.

Furthermore, U.S. imperialism has to grapple with a militant anti-imperialism that characterizes contemporary India. Both Coca-Cola and Pepsi discovered this to their unease when both were accused of abusing Indian water resources. As *Business Week* saw it, this was of a piece with a global trend: once "foreign companies...transformed oil, diamonds and countless other raw materials into profits that flow from developing nations to wealthy ones. Now the playing field is leveling," it concluded mournfully—and correctly.[41]

Boeing, a major defense contractor, now employs hundreds of Indians who are writing software for next-generation cockpits, and building systems to prevent airborne collisions. The pharmaceutical Eli Lilly, which has major rivals in India (who have profited handsomely from collaboration with their Cuban counterparts, part of that nation's world class health care system), is now seeking to collaborate with companies there. U.S. based Cisco Systems, whose operations are essential to the smooth functioning of the all-important Internet, has decided that 20% of its top talent should be in India within five years. As of December 2007, Accenture, the leading U.S. based consulting firm, had more employees in India than in the U.S. itself. Citicorp, the mega-bank based in Manhattan, is moving in a similar direction, as is IBM.[42] GM is in the process of buying as much as $1 billion worth of car parts in India annually and plans to double its production capacity in India to 225,000 vehicles a year by making more product at its Halol factory in the state of Gujarat and building a new plant in Talegaon, Maharashtra, both in western India.[43] The latest news is that editing, post-production and archiving services of the world's media companies—Fox, TIME-Warner, Disney, etc.—will be migrating to India. The outsourcing specialist Genpact—40% owned by General Electric—is behind this.[44]

This is not just a response to lower wages in India—though that certainly is a factor—but more than this it is a response to a geo-strategic imperative of the U.S. ruling class, which has decided that not only has there been undue U.S. reliance on China but, as well, an alternative to China must be built up. Secretary of State Condoleeza Rice put it bluntly when she said U.S. policy was to "help" India become a world power—hence, nuclear cooperation. What she did not say was this was not because of altruism towards South Asians but that this dovetails with the gathering idea to blunt China's rise. Washington's problem is that India is not willing to be a Yankee satrap and thus is determined to pursue construction of a $9 billion pipeline that would connect South Asia with Iranian gas fields, a putative violation of the 1996 Iran-Libya Sanctions Act.[45] However this sticky matter is resolved, the end result of this entente with India will be the further diminishing of U.S. imperialism.

Clearly the road will not be smooth. China retains a close relationship with Pakistan, a breeding ground for renegade warriors who have inflicted major damage in Indian Kashmir, bringing Delhi and Islamabad to the brink of war more than once. Yet the primary point is that the U.S. ruling elite is not united on the China Question—principally because of the large stake that Kodak, Motorola, GM, Microsoft and other behemoths have in China's economy, a situation unlike that involving the former Soviet Union.

This difficulty in drawing a bead on Beijing is no better exemplified than when one considers Pentagon planning against China. As recently as late 1999, the Joint Chiefs of Staff listed China as a potential future adversary—a development that the *Washington Post* characterized as a "momentous change from the last decade of the Cold War." Yet when the final version of the document, entitled "Joint Vision 2020" was released the next year, it was far more discreet. Rather than explicitly pointing the finger of indictment at China, it simply warned of the possible rise of an unidentified "peer competitor"—later this became a "rising large East Asian nation." No one dared to note the obvious: China was in the crosshairs, having served its purpose in bringing down the former Soviet Union, thank you very much. This was in the context of a shift away from the traditional focus on Europe; as the *Post* put it, "the Pentagon is looking at Asia as the most likely arena for future military conflict, or at least competition." (Unfortunately, scholars and critics in the humanities have failed to consider that the shift in the literary canon away from the "Eurocentric" curriculum is a reflection in the shift in imperialist strategy—and not solely the product of the demands of African-Americans particularly, the convenient whipping boy when white supremacy is compelled to engage in an agonizing retreat.)

Thus, the Pentagon has begun placing more attack submarines in the Pacific; more war games and strategic studies have been centered on Asia. Beginning in the 1990s there was an unannounced shift in the Navy's deployment of submarines generally, which have been critical in intercepting communications, monitoring ship movements and clandestinely inserting commandos—not to mention as platforms for launching Tomahawk cruise missiles. Beginning in the 1990s, the Pentagon stopped placing 60% of its attack boats in the Atlantic. More began to be placed in the Pacific. Conceptually, the Pentagon began to contemplate that the locus of U.S. military engagement in the 21st century would be in the region ranging from Baghdad to Tokyo. (This concept also underscores retrospectively the importance of a vast Russia, for as the land bridge between Europe and Asia, those obsessed with global domination—as is U.S. imperialism—perforce must dominate that 1/6 of the world's territory that was formerly known as the Soviet Union.)

And, yes, ongoing conflicts in Iraq and Afghanistan and pending war in Iran—all of which are sited in West Asia—have to be viewed in this context, just as the major conflicts of the second half of the 20th century that engaged U.S. imperialism were on the Korean peninsula and Indo-China, principally Vietnam. Indeed, a not coincidental aspect of the U.S. invasion of Iraq was to wipe out China's stakes in that nation's oilfields. Beijing had signed a $1.3 billion contract in 1997 to develop the Al-Ahdab field in central Iraq—but the U.S. occupation obliterated this deal.[46] This points up an unavoidable thesis: growing hostility to China is fueled by its growing challenge to U.S. imperialism in oil markets.

This is why as a new century dawned, Andrew Krepinevich, Director of the influential think-tank, the Center for Strategic and Budgetary Assessments, announced portentously that "the focus of great power competition is likely to shift from Europe to Asia," while James Bodner, then a Pentagon official, concurred adding that "the center of gravity of the world economy has shifted to Asia, and U.S. interests flow with that." (This is one reason why the resuscitation of Russia under Putin has been so maddening for U.S. imperialism, for strategically it is well-nigh impossible to focus on both Russia and China while embroiled in major conflicts in Iraq and Afghanistan—then Iran; this also underscores why the Pentagon must have an entente with India, while suppressing pacifist sentiments in Japan.)

Captivatingly, U.S. imperialism had a demonstration of what might befall their plans for China in the wake of the Spring 2001 takedown by Beijing of a U.S. spy plane—engaged in surveillance of Chinese territory. The plane had taken off from Okinawa and Japanese elites became increasingly nervous as the standoff unfolded. Seoul was nervous thinking that rising tensions could undermine their long-range plans of Korean reunification.[47] As the *Washington Post* archly put it, "with friends like these.....," who needs enemies. "Vocal support for the U.S. position was notably absent"—particularly there was "Japan's tepid, ambiguous stance." The "motto of the East Asian governments appears to be that they will always stand behind the United States—about as far behind as they can get." [48] Even U.S. trans-national companies were unnerved by it all. Motorola, with 12,000 employees and $3.4 billion tied up in China, was flustered, as were other big investors, e.g. Procter and Gamble and GM.[49]

It is unclear if the Pentagon drew sober lessons from this episode, recognizing that allies and U.S. businesses alike were not necessarily enthusiastic about an increase in bellicosity toward Beijing. After the crisis was resolved, then Secretary of Defense, Donald Rumsfeld, cut off virtually all of the Pentagon's contacts with the Chinese armed forces, which could only engender suspicions and bad feelings.[50]

Of late, suspicion of the Chinese military has risen on this side of the Pacific. Beijing has been accused by the Pentagon of modernizing and expanding its arsenal of nuclear weapons, giving it enhanced nuclear strike capability.[51] The Pentagon asserts that Beijing is increasing deployment of mobile land and sea-based ballistic nuclear missiles that have the range to hit the U.S.[52] This is said to include a new class of submarine that threatens the nuclear balance by providing Beijing with a more robust nuclear deterrent.[53] Several Chinese residents of Los Angeles were arrested and charged with providing Beijing with defense technology from the U.S. Navy.[54] A U.S. General declared that China is seeking to unseat the U.S. as the dominant power in cyberspace—as part of asymmetrical warfare that would involve e.g. hacking into and disabling Pentagon computers.[55] The unrealistic U.S. imperialists continue to urge Taiwan—which Beijing continues to see as a rebel province—to take steps toward independence; the *Washington Times*, foremost among these reactionaries, suggested that this crisis may mean that China "will be forced to go to war with the United States." [56] At the GOP convention in 2000, there was a bitter battle about a plank that would have called for U.S. diplomatic recognition of Taiwan—a gross provocation in Beijing's eyes.[57] To the dismay of these crazies, Taiwan—with a population of about 20 million—is being economically integrated into China, whose population is more than 50 times larger.

One would have thought that Armageddon was nigh when China

displayed the ability to shoot down a satellite—of course, only U.S. imperialism should have this capability. Quickly retaliating, State Department bureaucrats curtly informed Asia Satellite Telecommunications, a Hong Kong based and listed regional satellite operator, that a plan to take the company private would jeopardize its future access to the U.S. satellite technology—on which its business depends. Dismissed was the fact that General Electric has a major stake in this enterprise.[58] More persuasive was the earlier report that China's military had deployed a new reconnaissance satellite that could conceivably target U.S. forces in the region[59] and that technology from Hong Kong could leak to the mainland.

The specter of Chinese spying has erupted, reminiscent of 1930s propaganda that played upon bigoted stereotypes of "sneaky" Japanese. During the Clinton Administration this atmosphere ensnared Wen Ho Lee, a scientist of Taiwanese extraction toiling in New Mexico, who was charged and prosecuted in the press for atomic espionage on behalf of Beijing (in an updated replay of what led to the execution of Julius and Ethel Rosenberg in the early 1950s)—before being exonerated.[60] It is almost as if U.S. imperialism finds it hard to believe that any Chinese on this side of the Pacific would sympathize with a nation grounded in white supremacy, but would sympathize automatically with a nation whose avowed aim is the construction of the foundations of socialism. Unsurprisingly, an official investigation found that there was pervasive racial profiling in the Energy Department that victimized Asian-Americans and made for a "hostile work environment" and subsequent "brain drain." As the perceptive journalist, Joe Conason, saw it, this Asian-bashing was part of a larger scheme by conservatives to paint their Democratic foes as soft on China and in thrall to Beijing. This was during the time when the Clinton White House was being battered by saucy allegations concerning Charlie Trie's donations to the President's legal expense trust, alleged illegal fund-raising for the Democrats by John Huang and the like.[62]

Though France is known to be a past master at industrial espionage, about one-third of all economic espionage investigations in the U.S. involve China.[63] "Such economic espionage threatens the foundations of U.S. prosperity, say current and former counterintelligence officials," according to the hyperbolic *USA Today*.[64]

Yet the problem faced by U.S. imperialism is that the quagmire it has created in Iraq and Afghanistan limits severely its ability to confront China—and its North Korean ally. Two top U.S. military commanders have admitted as much.[65]

Perhaps more worrisome is the fact that although no Asian NATO has arisen as of yet, the embryo of an Asian Warsaw Pact is up and running. It was in 1996, shortly after a tense confrontation between the U.S. and China in the Taiwan Straits—which led to bellicose warnings of a Chinese military leader about bombarding Los Angeles—that the Shanghai Cooperation Organization began to take shape.[66] In 2001 it was organized formally with China and Russia at the helm. Splitting Beijing from Moscow was fundamental in the U.S. "triumphing" in the Cold War conflict with the Soviet Union. Their unity—and particularly the increased ties between these two powers—presents a challenge as formidable as any presented to U.S. imperialism in the past half-century. Iran also has been associated with this grouping, as has India and Pakistan—which may serve to curb their bilateral tensions. In turn official sources in Beijing and Moscow blasted U.S. imperialism's designs on Teheran in no uncertain terms. On 13 April 2006 the *People's Daily* in Beijing charged that plans on regime change by Washington were at the root of the crisis and the nuclear issue was mere camouflage, while Gennady Yefstafiyev, a former General in Russia's Foreign Intelligence Service was even blunter, charging that U.S. imperialism desired "control over Iran's oil and gas" and desired further to "use its territory as the shortest route for the transportation of hydrocarbons under U.S. control from the regions of Central Asia and the Caspian Sea bypassing Russia and China." Naturally, Washington was rebuffed when it sought observer status at the SCO summit.[67]

As if that were not a sufficient challenge, U.S. imperialism's policy toward China is increasingly being confronted at home. Writing for the *People's Weekly World* recently, John Wojcik noted that a new battle is unfolding with Wal-Mart, Google, GE and other transnational corporations on one side and on the other are "workers' rights forces in China, including the All-China Federation of Trade Unions," joined by "labor and human rights groups in the U.S. and around the world." The issue concerns pro-labor legislation in Beijing, stoutly resisted by Big Business—and backed by unions globally. Unions' efforts have been joined by progressive members of Congress, including U.S. Representative Barbara Lee of Oakland. This international worker solidarity may be a sign of things to come.[68]

Thus, the trillions spent on subduing the Soviet Union have not led to global domination by U.S. imperialism, for this plot involved a deal with China that has gone sour; more than this, China is poised to surge into the front ranks of nations with consequences so awesome for U.S. imperialism and its adhesive, white supremacy, that the consequences have yet to be tallied.

4: Cuba Sí, Yanqui No

Ramon Ripoll Diaz was pleased.

And why shouldn't he be? As members of a sizeable delegation from China assembled before this First Deputy Minister of the Ministry of Foreign Investment and Economic Cooperation of Cuba, he happily signed a document that would mean increased trade between his nation and this Asian giant. Though many in Washington had predicted that Socialist Cuba would collapse in the wake of the 1991 collapse of the Soviet Union, this did not occur, not only because of the sweat and toil and ideological rigor of the Cubans themselves, led by the Communist Party, but also because of aid and trade with Venezuela—and China. In 2006 alone the total value of trade between China and Cuba rose to $2.181 billion, double the figure for 2005. China had donated critical teaching materials but, perhaps more important was the fact that beginning in 2001 Cuba began broad trade in technology with the Asian titan when Beijing granted the island a credit for improving telecommunications, which greatly benefited telephone services, radio transmissions and informatics. More visible on the island are the thousands of modern Yutong buses that are now transporting passengers from one province to another and the household electrical appliances—not unlike those that dot modern U.S. households from the same source. In turn Cuba has been exporting sugar, nickel and PPG, a medication to combat excess cholesterol, to China.[1]

The continued vigor of Socialist Cuba has not been greeted with equanimity by U.S. imperialism. Beginning in 1959, Washington sought to strangle this radical infant in its cradle and, failing that, sought to murder President Fidel Castro hundreds of times, an effort that distorted politics in the U.S., particularly in Southern Florida. Thus, seeking to incite a new Cold War, of late U.S. imperialism has been warning luridly about how China—allegedly—is "shipping arms and explosives to Cuba" and the presumed threat this presented to amorphous U.S. "interests."[2]

Yet despite the repeated attempts to undermine Havana, repeatedly in multi-lateral bodies, e.g. the United Nations, the militant island has received increasing support in its effort to end the blockade by U.S. imperialism. Cuba's growing prestige is buoyed by its own massive foreign aid program, particularly to smaller nations in Latin America and Africa. Immediately after the disaster that was Hurricane Katrina in 2005, the Cuban government immediately offered assistance to the U.S., promising that it would send 1600 doctors and 36 tons of medical supplies. Washington adamantly refused this generosity—though, perhaps, the 1800 persons who did die as a result of this catastrophe may have been saved but for this ideological blindness. Nonplussed, Havana then self-lessly offered to donate the substantial sum it won in the World Baseball Classic to victims of Katrina.[3]

Yet Cuba's unselfishness was nothing new. Havana established its first international medical brigade in 1963 and dispatched 58 doctors and health workers to newly independent Algeria. From that moment until 2005, more than 100,000 doctors and health workers intervened in 97 nations, mostly in Africa and Latin America. By March 2006, 25,000 Cuban professionals were working in 68 nations. This is more than even the World Health Organization can deploy, while Medicins Sans Frontieres sent only 2040 doctors and nurses abroad in 2003, and 2290 in 2004. No other government, private body or international organization has managed to put together a global medical program on such a scale as Cuba's, or to offer such a a level of assistance to those in need of care. Cuba has pioneered in fighting the HIV-AIDS pandemic and countless lives have been saved worldwide—notably in Africa—as a result.

It is principally because of the example of Cuba that Latin America as a whole—notably Bolivia, Ecuador, Chile, Argentina, Venezuela, Nicaragua, Brazil, etc.—has moved decisively to the left; Havana's aid cannot be discounted in illuminating this turn. There are currently some 14,000 Cuban doctors working in poverty-stricken areas of Venezuela. A few hours before he took up office as President of Bolivia in December 2005, Evo Morales signed his first international treaty, which was with Cuba, setting up a joint unit to offer free ophthamological treatment. As well as a national institute in this complex field in La Paz, recently equipped by Cuba, there will be medical centers in the cities of Cochabamba and Santa Cruz. Young Bolivians will also have the opportunity to join thousands of other foreigners studying to become physicians at Cuba's Latin American School of Medicine.

Again, U.S. imperialism is fearful of the example set by Socialist Cuba, especially—once more—for Havana shows what the *public sector* can do in the critically important realm of medicine: service is free of charge, which is antithetical to—and subversive of—the for profit model that dominates in Washington.[4] The progressive filmmaker, Michael Moore, pointed out the "health care and insurance industry....is a major corporate underwriter of ...George Bush and the Republican Party, having contributed over $13 million to [his] presidential campaign in 2004 and more than $180 million to Republican candidates over the last two campaign cycles."[5] Conservatives and their plutocratic backers feel that they will be the biggest losers if Socialist Cuba continues to thrive—and they very well may be correct.

But the real losers today are millions of people in the U.S. and elsewhere who will continue to suffer as long as the Cuban model is not emulated. The progressive analyst, Sarah van Gelder, pointed out that Cubans "live longer than almost anyone in Latin America. Far fewer babies die. Almost everyone has been vaccinated, and such scourges of the poor as parasites, TB, malaria, even HIV/AIDS are rare or nonexistent.....Cubans no longer suffer from diphtheria, rubella, polio, or measles......Cuban researchers develop their own vaccinations and treatments..... Anyone can see a doctor...right in the neighborhood."[6]

This living example of what socialism means has endeared Cubans to Africans particularly. On his second official visit to Cuba in the Spring of 2001, South African President Thabo Mbeki bedecked Havana with fulsome praise, especially since the island hosts 180 South African students and has dispatched 463 doctors to toil in Mbeki's nation, chiefly in poor, rural zones.[7] Mbeki was notably pleased by Cuba's initiative in producing low-cost drugs for the HIV-AIDS pandemic, which has devastated South Africa. Here Havana fearlessly decided to cross swords with the large pharmaceutical corporations headquartered in the U.S. who are poised to profit from the misery of poor Africans. During this same visit Castro and Mbeki signed agreements in maritime commerce, air services, sports, culture and science and technology, all of which served to strengthen South Africa's government.[8] Even the Australian-American, James Wolfensohn, who formerly headed the World Bank, felt compelled to assert that Cuba had done a "'great job'" in attending to the welfare of its people. This was said after the Spring 2001 publication of the Bank's statistics showing Cuba topping virtually all other poor nations in health and education. Other senior Bank officials went further and suggested that other developing nations should seek to emulate Cuba—though, like North Korea, Cuba has not received a penny in Bank aid, at least not since 1960. Unlike U.S. imperialism, the World Bank chose not to ignore the reality that by 1997 there were 12 primary pupils for every Cuban teacher, a ratio that compared favorably with Sweden's.[9]

Nevertheless, a growing segment of the U.S. ruling elite wants to do business with Socialist Cuba and are tired of losing out to their European and Asian competitors. In the Spring of 2007 Cuba was slated to sign deals worth $150 million with U.S. food producers.[10] Many U.S. firms hunger to do more business with Socialist Cuba and millions more would like to see the criminal blockade ended. As the *Los Angeles Times* put it, "farmers want to sell more produce [to Cuba], oil companies want to explore Cuba's gulf deposits, and the travel industry anticipates a million U.S. visitors to Cuba the first year it is legal." The Cuban Reconciliation Act, sponsored by Congressman Jose E. Serrano of the Bronx—who happens to be of Puerto Rican descent—proposes to lift the 45-year old trade embargo. Congressman Bill Delahunt of Massachusetts has submitted a bill to rescind restrictions on Cuban Americans' visits to family on the island, now limited to once every other three years. A bill submitted by Congressman Jerry Moran of Kansas—who, unlike Serrano and Delahunt, is a Republican—aims to ease the payment regimen for agricultural sales to Cuba, which have been legal since 2000 but have been stifled by the U.S. authorities.[11] The USA Rice Federation, based in Arlington, Virginia, opposes the Treasury Department's regulations requiring Cuba to make upfront payments for U.S. goods—e.g. rice—which hinders such sales.[12] A growing number of members of Congress are objecting to key elements of the anti-Havana crusade, notably Radio and TV Marti, which over two decades have soaked up more than a half billion dollars in U.S. government funds, while garnering fewer than 100,000 listeners and viewers on the island of 12 million.[13] Twenty Miami based groups that, quite frankly, are enemies of the Cuban Revolution—including the otherwise odious Cuban American National Foundation—were calling on the White House to end the restrictions on travel and remittances to Cuba.[14]

As the financial meltdown accelerates in the U.S., spurred by the "cowboy capitalism" that has become endemic, there will be increasing cries for normalizing relations—particularly economic relations—with Socialist Cuba. A report by the U.S. International Trade Commission asserts that eliminating restrictions on trade and travel to Cuba could double agricultural exports to the island.[15]

Yet the Bush White House, true to its troglodyte nature, has sought to increase hostility toward Havana. Shortly after taking office, George W. Bush ordered tougher enforcement of long-standing sanctions against Cuba and promised to extend support to so-called "dissidents" there.[16] Reputedly, the U.S. Treasury Department has more agents devoted to monitoring Cuba than "terrorists." This anti-Havana attitude was reflected in early appointments to the State Department, e.g. Otto Reich, a notorious Cuban exile, who even the ever cautious *New York Times* conceded was "at odds with farmers, business executives and a growing number of members of Congress-including many Republicans—who have been pushing for trade with Cuba." [17]

Academia, traditionally more inclined toward enlightened views than other sectors in the U.S., also has objected to the hard-line toward

Havana. Thus, it was not surprising when the "Emergency Coalition to Defend Educational Travel," a group of about 450 faculty members and other higher-educational professionals sued in federal court the Treasury Department and its Office of Foreign Assets Control, challenging travel restrictions imposed by the Bush team in 2004 that virtually ended academic travel to the island. However, in a remarkable repudiation of the supposed constitutional right to travel, their reasonable lawsuit was rejected.[18] The difficulty involved in journeying to Cuba was revealed by filmmaker, Michael Moore, when he was investigated by Washington as a result of his trip there.[19]

One of the many reasons for U.S. imperialism's belligerence towards Socialist Cuba is Havana's support for Puerto Rican sovereignty and independence. Cuban patriots historically have seen the two islands as "two wings of the same bird" and both came under U.S. hegemony as a result of the jingoistic 1898 war against a tottering Spanish colonial empire. Thus, Washington is not happy with being dragged into the Inter-American Commission on Human Rights of the Organization of American States, where it is being forced to justify why their colonial subjects in Puerto Rico are deprived of effective voting rights.[20] The Puerto Rican Independence Party has won more adherents of late because of its staunch defense of the homeland, particularly in the aftermath of the assassination of independence activist, Filiberto Ojeda Rios on 23 September 2006.[21] U.S. imperialism realizes that a free Puerto Rico would further bolster Socialist Cuba.

The very existence of a Cuba that has escaped the clutches of neo-colonialism smooths the path for other smaller nations in the region to exercise sovereignty and improve the well-being of their citizenry. When the progressive forces in Jamaica were dislodged in the Summer 2007 and replaced by their conservative opponents, the latter—unlike the case earlier when they shunned Havana—reassured Socialist Cuba they would like to continue high-level cooperation, including the provision of medical assistance.[22] Kingston may have taken sober note of the disturbing report that the personal assistant of the top general in the California National Guard has been placed on leave after revelations that the aide's personal web-site referred to Jamaicans as "cannibals."[23]

On the other hand, escalating hostility toward Socialist Cuba has been the norm since the advent of the wild-eyed Bush team. Yet for decades since 1959, there have been numerous bombings in Cuba—and South Florida—executed by diehards unwilling to accept that their time has passed. As one commentator put it, "Back in the '60s, some Cubans were trained like Bin Laden;" he was referring to e.g the 1973 bombing of the headquarters of a Miami magazine, deemed to be insufficiently hostile to Havana; a 1966 bombing in which a Miami radio commentator lost his legs; and countless other acts of terrorism.[24]

Thus, it was not overly surprising when the U.S. Fifth Circuit Court of Appeals in New Orleans freed Luis Posada Carriles in the Spring of 2007—a man the *Los Angeles Times* called "the Zacarias Moussaoui of Havana and Caracas," referring to the so-called "20th hijacker" of September 11th. Posada, 79, has been credibly accused of blowing up a Cuban civilian airliner that killed scores of innocents—yet he has been treated with kid gloves by the U.S. authorities.[25] Understandably, Havana was irate, charging correctly that "the U.S. government has maliciously violated not only Resolution No. 1373 (2001) of the United Nations Security Council, a resolution prompted by [Washington], but also treaties on terrorism to which it is a signatory, most especially the International Convention for the Suppression of Terrorist Bombings, which became effective on May 23, 2001 and the Convention for the Suppression of Unlawful Acts Against the Safety of Civil Aviation, which went into effect on January 26, 1973." [26]

It is not surprising that a fed-up Havana eventually felt compelled to dispatch emissaries to the U.S. as a way to halt this terrorism being launched with—minimally—the tacit approval of Washington. Ultimately, these men—now known globally as the "Cuban Five"—were arrested and jailed in the U.S.; as the *Chicago Tribune* later put it, "one of Cuba's most celebrated spies was born in a flat along Chicago's bustling Ashland Avenue in 1956" but "after his parents returned home to Cuba in 1961......[Rene] Gonzalez grew up to become a Cuban agent." [27] It is as if U.S. imperialism does not want to stop terrorism against Socialist Cuba—and doesn't want Havana to do so either.

The retrograde attitude of U.S. imperialism toward Socialist Cuba has won Washington few friends, least of all in the hemisphere where even neighboring Canada has repudiated this nonsensical approach. Ottawa long has had diplomatic relations with Socialist Cuba and their revered leader, the late Pierre Trudeau, was known to be a personal friend of Fidel Castro. The forward-looking attitude of Ottawa is suggestive of how isolated U.S. imperialism has become; though evidently oblivious, Washington made what was termed an "unprecedented foray into Canada's election campaign" in January 2006. Quite rightly, Canadians worry when they see a neighbor engaged in dangerous and provocative activities, knowing that the fires left unchecked could reach their shores. Thus, Ottawa has been critical of the laggard approach by U.S. imperialism toward climate change and the Kyoto treaty, the criminal occupation of Iraq and sticky bilateral issues, e.g. tariffs on Canadian soft lumber. This brought a stiff rebuke from Washington but, as elsewhere, U.S. imperialism is wildly unpopular north of the border.[28] Matters were not helped when, extraordinarily, a majority of the U.S. Senate demanded limited Canadian access to the U.S. market for lumber.[29] Subsequently, this same august U.S. Senate voted to block the importation of Canadian cattle into the U.S. market.[30] Of late Ottawa and Washington have clashed about the former's Arctic claims, which the latter—with the acceleration of global warming—seeing the melting of ice and the concomitant creation of the fabled "Northwest Passage" as a short-cut to the markets of Asia (through territorial waters claimed by Canada). This has caused Ottawa to beef up its military in this now contested region, suggesting how the very existence of U.S. imperialism distorts the priorities and harms the well-being of even those thought to be allies.[31]

Mexico could provide first-hand testimony about this salient point. It was in 1846 that the U.S. seized 25% of that nation's territory—including California—in a war of aggression. This after being blocked from seizing Canada during the War of 1812—and winding up with the White House in flames, events that inspired the bellicose U.S. national anthem. Now as a direct result of the so-called North American Free Trade Agreement (NAFTA), Mexican farmers and agricultural workers are being forced off the soil and compelled to migrate northward where they face an uncertain fate. Between 2000 and 2005 Mexico lost an estimated 900,000 jobs in the countryside and 700,000 in the cities as NAFTA began to bite. After NAFTA, six million Mexicans came to live in the U.S. This has become a major political matter with conservatives—like former GOP presidential candidate Pat Buchanan—sounding the alarm about what he sees as the potent demographic and political impact of these migrants.[32] The most recent book from KKK and Nazi leader David Duke—who received the majority of the Euro-American vote in a race for Governor of Louisiana in 1991—also has engaged in vile immigrant-bashing, focusing on Mexicans.[33]

Yet Buchanan and his cowardly comrades would be well-advised to point the finger at NAFTA. The *Houston Chronicle*, not regarded as a beacon of progressivism, could not avoid noticing that "much of Mexico's farm country has been overwhelmed by an influx of crops from the United States in the years following [NAFTA]. Over the next two years," it was announced in early 2007, "the final provisions of the trade pact kick in, opening Mexico to unlimited imports of poultry from its northern neighbor." Unavoidably, those driven off the land will seek greener pastures elsewhere—e.g. in Houston, Chicago, Los Angeles and New York City.[34] *Indian Country Today*, a journal based in New York state, but which monitors carefully the well-being of hemispheric indigenes, pointed out that the indigenous were over-represented among Mexican migrants and their movement north was a direct result of a "failed exercise in open-market globalization." [35] Increasingly, the corpses of Mexican migrants have been found in the parched deserts of southern Arizona, dead testaments to the danger posed by NAFTA. [36]

With certain state legislatures on the warpath against Mexican migrant workers, their numbers have been reduced. So now Colorado farmers have signed a contract with the prison authorities that could supply them 10-member crews of low-security female prisoners to do the labor that migrants once performed—though it is hard to believe, prison labor may be cheaper, [37] an abject lesson in how immigrant-bashing serves to pave the path for further exploitation of the U.S. working class. Actually, the influx of migrants from Mexico has served to erode the dominance of conservatism, for when they gain citizenship and vote, this group is likely to cast their ballots like those of their African-American brothers and sisters, an indication of their historic close ties that no amount of prodding can shake. [38] Fortunately, more Mexican migrants are moving to Georgia, Virginia and North Carolina, bastions of rock-ribbed conservatism, desperately in need of more progressive elements. [39]

Yet the draconian measures taken against Mexicans, e.g. building a wall along the 2000 mile long border that separates their nation from the U.S., are destined to backfire. As Shannon O'Neil of the elite Council on Foreign Relations observed, "the immigration concern of the future will be how to entice Mexicans and other Latin Americans to cross into the U.S. in the numbers [needed]." As she sees it, "Mexico is undergoing a demographic transition," involving smaller families in an economy to be buoyed by increasing Japanese, Brazilian and Indian investment; similarly, the U.S. population is becoming older and may require an influx from Mexico to stay afloat. Anti-Mexican attitudes do not bode well for the future, she maintains. [40]

Immigrant-bashing elides the point that this praxis compromises—ultimately—the ability of U.S. nationals to eat, in that agriculture in this nation has become so heavily dependent upon migrant labor. This praxis should be supplanted by a dedicated campaign to improve the wages and working conditions of those toiling in the fields. What occurs in Immokalee, Florida, is a dramatic example of what faces thousands nationally. Arising in the dark at 4 a.m., hundreds of men head to a 12-hour work day, spent on their hands and knees, filling buckets of tomatoes for 40 to 50 cents a bucket. If it rains, work stops. Things have not changed much since the legendary journalist, Edward R. Murrow, produced his trailblazing television documentary "Harvest of Shame" which highlighted the despicable conditions in Immokalee. These workers continue to receive no benefits, nor job security, and work seven days a week.

These workers continue to live in hovels. Admittedly, since the Coalition of Immokalee Workers began to organize in 2001, things have improved somewhat. They launched a boycott of Taco Bell, a chain that is part of a giant corporation; but since slavery has been uncovered in this part of the "Sunshine State"—there is substantial room for improvement.[41]

Although there has been vociferous objection to the presence on these shores of struggling Mexican migrant laborers, less has been said about the influx of more affluent Latin Americans, fleeing social change in places like Venezuela. Yet, as early as the Summer of 2000, the *Miami Herald* noticed that tens of thousands were fleeing nations like Venezuela, Argentina and Ecuador, mostly to settle in South Florida, where they have augmented the conservative strength of certain Cuban-American elites. President Hugo Chavez had only been in office for a little more than a year, yet "about 150,000 Venezuelans" already had "left their country," with tens of thousands fleeing the anticipated backlash in Argentina engendered by reaction against U.S. puppet, Carlos Menem.[42]

In a sense, this flood of migrants fleeing the specter of progressivism could be counted as a contribution made to Latin America, as it reduces the possibility that these individuals could augment the dwindling number of reactionaries in the region. Thus, in the wake of the triumph of the overthrow of the Somoza dictatorship in Nicaragua, thousands from this nation fled to South Florida. And although some returned to their homeland, their presence was insufficient to block the return of Daniel Ortega of the Sandinistas to power. Today, he has joined hands with Havana and Caracas and has refused to kowtow to U.S. imperialism. He triumphed at the polls in 2006, though Washington blatantly interfered in the internal affairs of this sovereign state.[43]

The displacing of U.S. stooges in Managua has emboldened the Nicaraguan working class. It was after Ortega's election that workers toiling for Dole Food Co. on a banana plantation, sued their employer in a U.S. court charging that they were consciously exposed to a pesticide manufactured by Dow Chemical Co.—of napalm infamy during the war in Vietnam—that led to their being sterilized. These Nicaraguan workers have been joined by thousands of former banana workers from Costa Rica, Honduras, Guatemala and Panama. In addition to Dole and Dow, Del Monte Fresh Produce Inc., Chiquita Brands and Shell Oil Co. are named as defendants. Epidemiological studies have shown that the pesticide in question causes sterility in men, according to the U.S. Agency for Toxic Substances and Disease Registry. Again, their plight cannot be extricated from that of their fellow workers north of the border, for it was in 1977 when about three dozen factory workers at an Occidental Petroleum Corporation subsidiary in Lathrop, California, where this pesticide was used, reported problems having children.[44]

This pummeling of the Nicaraguan working class, a direct out-growth of the illegal "contra war" of the 1980s, has been the prelude for U.S. imperialism now branding Central America as the "New Asia"—or now ripe for plucking. "Near-sourcing" is the term used to describe what has descended on Nicaragua particularly—i.e. call centers and the like, this time targeting the U.S.'s burgeoning Spanish-speaking population. Since Managua is in the same time zone as many U.S. cities, it is seen as perfect in this regard and, thus, Dell Computer, IBM, Procter and Gamble and Western Union have installed facilities in the region, joined by man-ufacturers, e.g. Sara Lee. The pay—a meager $400 per month—is triple the minimum wage. Costa Rica also has been viewed as a site for this kind of exploitation, now that Managua's earlier attempt to embark on a non-capitalist path of development has been blocked—at least seemingly.[45]

Yet Costa Ricans have stunned Washington with the vehemence of their opposition to the Central American Free Trade Agreement [CAFTA]. It was in late September 2007 that more than 100,000 Costa Ricans, some dressed as skeletons, protested CAFTA, which they charged would flood their nation with cheap farm goods and cause job losses. Some protesters wore derisive masks of George W. Bush, as they railed against their nation joining other smaller nations in Central America in what they consider to be a suicide pact.[46]

Still, it is not accidental that oil companies—Shell and Occidental in the first place—have been implicated in Central American deviltry for their swashbuckling rapaciousness in lusting for super-profits has involved the trammeling and trampling of workers. Ecuador could well attest to this. In the Spring of 2007, this South American nation dispatched an attorney to meet with Governor Arnold Schwarznegger of California, seeking aid in pressing a lawsuit that alleges environmental damage inflicted by Chevron Corporation, a financial supporter of the Chief Executive of the Golden State, and a patron of U.S. Secretary of State Condoleeza Rice, who—quite appropriately, given her labors for Big Oil—named an oil tanker after her. Since the recall campaign of 2003 that ousted his Democratic Party predecessor, Gray Davis, Chevron has given a hefty $566,000 to the governor's coffers and donated $50,000 to help pay for his second inauguration. Then in June 2007 Chevron donated $250,000 to the state GOP, which aired television advertisements promot-ing his re-election. The governor, who spends an inordinate amount of time on ski slopes in Sun Valley, Idaho could not find the time to meet with Ecuador's lawyer.[47]

Ecuador, which also produces bananas in addition to possessing oil fields, has joined the anti-imperialist wave spearheaded by Cuba, then joined by Venezuela, as suggested by their attempted confrontation of Schwarznegger. Their leader, Rafael Correa, who has advanced degrees in economics, is insisting on the departure of the U.S. military from the Manta air base they now occupy. The presence of U.S. planes rankles Ecuadoreans who think their purpose is not to interdict the drug traffic but to keep a close eye on guerrillas in neighboring Colombia.[48] Troops and equipment at this base for subversion have quadrupled in the last few years and there is a palpable fear that it is being used—or could be used—for interference in the internal affairs of Quito's neighbors. The Cuban journalist, Lidice Valenzuela, has argued that "the idea of completely taking over Latin America constitutes part of the Pentagon's new strategic map, which would permit the so-called superpower to guarantee, in the near future—once free of trade barriers and geographic borders via the free trade agreements—certain products that are needed on a world scale, including oil...." In addition to Manta, the Pentagon controls "nine strategically located bases in the Caribbean and South America," while using the guise of fighting drugs, terrorism and the like.[49]

Surely, President Hugo Chavez of Venezuela is high on the hit-list of the Pentagon. This became clear during the abortive Caracas coup of the Spring of 2002 where the fingerprints of U.S. imperialism were evident. When a revived Chavez then moved to seize the Orinoco oil belt on behalf of the state, pulses raced further in Washington—and on Wall Street—for, again, there was the dreaded specter of an enhanced public sector haunting U.S. imperialism. Oil giants—Exxon-Mobil; Conoco-Phillips; Chevron; Total of France; and Britain's BP—had owned this Venezuelan patrimony but were now left to fume.[50] "Go-it-alone governments are choking back output to perilous levels," asserted an obviously peeved *Business Week*.[51]

From their point of view, it is bad enough for Caracas to reclaim what is rightfully theirs but, worse—as they see it—is Venezuela spreading the wealth via literacy programs, education and the like. For example, today Venezuela has some of the most advanced programs in music education in the world, which have produced world-class musicians that have benefited the U.S.—thus, Gustavo Dudamel, the 26 year old Venezuelan wunderkind, was recently appointed chief conductor of the Los Angeles Philharmonic.[52] But the beneficent Chavez also has spread the nation's largesse abroad. It was at his initiative that leaders of small Caribbean nations met in Jamaica in the Summer of 2005 to ink a series of agreements that provided oil at preferential terms. These Caribbean nations can pay via barter of services or goods; e.g. bananas, rice or sugar.[53] A stunned *Houston Chronicle* asserted that "in terms of direct government funding, the scale of Venezuela's commitments is unprecedented for a Latin

American country." When floods ravaged Bolivia in 2007, the U.S. provided $1.5 million in a planeload of supplies and cash. Caracas provided ten times as much—and that was only the beginning.[54]

It was well that Caracas has been so helpful since small Caribbean nations have been suffering under the domination of, first, European colonialism, then U.S. imperialism. When the Marxist, Cheddi Jagan, sought to break the chains of bondage in 1953, he was overthrown unceremoniously by London.[55] St. Lucia, which with a small population of 160,000 has produced two Nobel Laureates, was producing quite recently 128,000 metric tons of bananas, less than 1% of the world market but the source of 50% of the island's export earnings. Banana growing then employed 25,000. But as the grim reaper of "free trade"—more precisely neo-colonial hegemony—has exacted its wrath, banana output is now less than 40,000 tons and fewer than 3000 islanders are growing the fruit. Migration to Toronto, London and New York has hardly led to the improvement of the well-being of the St. Lucians who remain on the island.[56] Antigua, which is tinier still than St. Lucia, has sought to establish a gaming industry and received a WTO ruling that this was acceptable. But Washington has chosen to ignore this ruling—while piously demanding that WTO rulings in their favor be regarded as holy writ—which has not been popular in the region.[57]

The militant influence of Caracas has extended south as well. Mapuche indigenes in Argentina have fought the illegal takeover of their land by two U.S. oil and gas companies: Pioneer Natural Resources and Apache Corporation. Chevron and Halliburton, who also operate in Argentina, have taken due note.[58]

Buenos Aires, traditionally a regional power, has allied with Caracas. Argentina remains angry at U.S. imperialism because of its support of the disastrous Carlos Menem and before that the military dictatorship of the late 1970s and 1980s, which pioneered in "disappearing" its citizens. Then despite the alliance between the Argentine right and U.S. imperialism, Buenos Aires still could not count on Washington during its war with London over the Malvinas [Falklands] Islands. Now Buenos Aires is joining with Caracas in establishing a regional bank to challenge the prerogatives of the International Monetary Fund, dominated by Washington and Brussels. Caracas has purchased about $3 billion in Argentine bonds, this after purchasing $25 million in Ecuadorean debt in 2005.[59] The Bank of the South has also received backing from Bolivia, Paraguay and possibly Nicaragua and Brazil[60] and, along with Telesur—Caracas' challenge to CNN and the BBC—has not made Caracas many friends in Washington. Caracas has angered U.S. imperialism further by having its state oil company convert its investment accounts from dollars to euros and Asian currencies. Adding insult to injury, President Chavez charged that the dollar is now encased in a "bubble"—that is bound to burst.[61]

Caracas has negotiated arms deals with Russia and has pledged to ship more of its oil to China. (Beijing opposed Washington when it backed Caracas' abortive attempt in 2006 to gain a seat at the UN Security Council.)[62] But most egregious in the eyes of U.S. imperialism may be its close ties to Iran. In Ciudad Bolivar on the banks of the Orinoco River in Venezuela, the two nations are collaborating in producing bright-red tractors; this will be followed by a bus factory and a cement plant. Teheran has pledged to invest a sizeable $9 billion in 125 projects in Venezuela, including constructing thousands of housing units.[63]

Like progressives in neighboring Colombia, Caracas has reached out to the pivotal constituency in the U.S.—African-Americans. Venezuela is collaborating with actor and activist Danny Glover in producing a film on the Haitian Revolution and has sought avidly to uplift the Afro-Venezuelan population—Chavez gained a spectacular near unanimous vote among this sector. Delegations of African-Americans now visit Caracas routinely.[64]

Caracas' tight alliance with Havana has reinforced both regimes. Similarly, this has forced U.S. imperialism to seek an accommodation with Brazil—larger in territory than the continental U.S. itself, with a population approaching 200 million. Like Caracas, relations between Brasilia and Beijing have proceeded spectacularly, with joint lofting of satellites being their latest venture.[65] Brazil's CVRD is the world's largest iron ore producer and this important commodity is pouring into Chinese ports in profusion, fueling the latter nation's booming steel plants.[66] Brazil also makes small planes—the Embraer, used on medium jaunts by Continental Airlines and other U.S. based airlines—and also a frequent sight in China. Though U.S. imperialism—as in Argentina—backed a military regime in the recent past in Brazil, now this malignant force is compelled to appear to be on friendly terms with the Social Democrats who presently reign in Brasilia. Washington's strategic objective is to drive a wedge between Brasilia, on the one hand, and Caracas-Havana on the other—so far, to no avail. For the Bush team did not make many friends in Brasilia when it slapped tariffs on steel imports in order to placate the captains of this industry, but which was a body blow to the Brazilian industry.[67] Other Brazilians are displeased with U.S. imperialism since GM and Ford particularly buy pig iron from the South American nation, which depends on charcoal, which in turn is leading to the devastating of the rain forests of the Amazon—all of which depends on the labor of virtual slaves living in unimaginable conditions in veritable forced-labor camps.[68]

Progressive Peruvians also are in dispute with U.S. imperialism. This reality was dramatized in Los Angeles during the Spring of 2007 when the mostly corpulent shareholders of Occidental Petroleum had their celebration of super-profits rudely interrupted by visitors from Peru. They accused the oil company of causing, and then ignoring, pervasive health and environmental problems in a remote region of the Amazon where Occidental has drilled for three decades. As one Peruvian put it balefully, "We are dying because of the contamination you caused in our lands. We cannot get the fish; we cannot drink the water. It's all toxic. You, Oxy, need to clean up the mess you left." [69]

Still, more consistent with the foreign policy of U.S. imperialism is what is occurring in Colombia, a nation that Washington plundered over a century ago when it induced Panama—then a part of this South American nation—to secede so that a canal could be built and then administered by the Yankees. It is in Colombia, a nation wracked by violence of startling proportions that the depredations of U.S. imperialism come clear. For Colombia is not only the site of a bloody war in which Washington is deeply enmeshed, it is also viewed as an essential component of U.S. imperialism's dream for "Free Trade in the Americas"—or the leveraged takeover of the entire hemisphere, a vision that stretches back to the addled vision of the Monroe Doctrine of almost two centuries ago. Fortunately, some in Congress have been repulsed by the close ties between President Alvaro Uribe and death squads, who recruited pop star Shakira to back him. Well, it may be true that "hips don't lie," as the Colombian pop princess has reminded us repeatedly, but the same cannot be said of the supposed benefit to the working class to be brought by "free trade"—certainly that is the viewpoint of the AFL-CIO.[70] The same can be said of the similarly heralded CAFTA or US-Central American Free Trade Agreement—or son of NAFTA. In fact, U.S. imperialism's accelerated push toward "free trade"—a misnomer if there ever was one—has been impelled by apprehension of European integration: Washington and Wall Street feel they must "integrate" all of the Americas in order to remain competitive. In turn, Brazil has led the charge for South American integration via MERCOSUR and Venezuela has pushed its progressive "Bolivarian Alternative" or ALBA—each of which is a gauntlet cast-down to U.S. imperialism.

The travails of the banana stalwart, Chiquita Brands, gives a hint of what is in store for the hemisphere if they open their doors wider to the intrusion of U.S. imperialism. Consider Roderick Hills, 76, a card-carrying member of the GOP establishment and a member of the Board of Chiquita. He had oversight of the company's "protection payments" to right-wing death squads in Colombia—who have specialized in murdering trade union leaders. His problem is that such payments were putative violations of U.S. law and his declining days may be spent behind bars. Chiquita's subsidiary in Colombia, Banadex, was this sprawling company's most profitable branch, and protecting the reliable flow of profits was Hills' primary concern. Hills, not going down by himself, argues that he kept U.S. authorities apprised of what he was doing and that they were happy to receive the intelligence his unsavory right-wing Colombian allies provided.[71] The militias paid by Chiquita are deeply involved in drug dealing and are of a piece with "Plan Colombia," Washington's multi-billion dollar initiative which is—supposedly—designed to bring to an end the attempt by the left-wing of Colombia to bring justice to their homeland using any means necessary, including the use of arms.[72]

The right-wing militias, however, are the chief reason why more trade unionists are murdered each year in Colombia than in the rest of the world combined; 72 such killings occurred in Colombia in 2006, and during President Uribe's blood-drenched tenure more than 400 worker advocates have been slaughtered, but only 10 convictions have ensued for these crimes.[73] Since 1991, 2262 unionists have been killed, which has prepared the battlefield for the incursions of Chiquita and other U.S. based trans-national corporations.[74]

One in the latter category is Drummond Ltd. of Birmingham, Alabama, now accused of aiding in the murder of labor leaders. Lawyers from the United Steelworkers and the International Labor Rights Fund are suing Drummond on behalf of the families of three Colombia union leaders who were killed by a right-wing paramilitary group. Founded in 1935, Drummond has become one of the nation's largest coal producers—and a prime culprit in the rise in global warming. At La Loma, Colombia this company operates the world's largest open-pit coal mine, extracting about 25 million tons of coal each year. Beginning in 1993—coincidentally as propaganda accelerated about the alleged need for the U.S. to fight drug traffickers in Colombia—the company solicited support from Bogota's military, donating land at its mine and port for bases, and lending vehicles, fuel, food and other supplies.[75] As in Iraq, Colombia also has proven to be a boondoggle for firms that supply mercenaries.[76] While the world has been riveted on U.S. imperialism's "blood for oil" crusade in Iraq, slipping under the radar has been their "blood for coal" crusade in Colombia.

U.S. unions are justifiably concerned that turning a blind eye to the murder of union leaders in one part of the hemisphere provides fertile grounds for such practices arising in another part. "Free trade" may well become a "free" transmission path of murderous tactics. But U.S. imperialism is desperate, faced as it is by a resolute Cuba whose example influences the entire hemisphere—but it is also concerned that the European

Union provides competition so stiff that it can only be met by Washington swallowing all of the Americas, thereby giving further resonance to the egotism that causes this North American nation to refer to itself simply as "America."

5: Europe Bites Back

Ronald Spogil was angry.

Unfortunately for this U.S. Ambassador to Rome, his outburst in the Spring of 2007 only fortified the image in the mind of many Europeans that U.S. imperialism was—once more—seeking to treat them as if he were the Viceroy of the continent. What had stoked the ire of Italians was his tirade against the Center-Left regime of Prime Minister Romano Prodi, because his government was seen in Washington as not being sufficiently welcome to a flood of U.S. capital, especially in the strategically critical telecommunications sector. In Rome, the Ambassador was seen as little more than a stalking horse for Rupert Murdoch, who conveniently had ditched his Australian nationality for that of the U.S., so as to better build his Fox-TV channel and related business interests (most recently the *Wall Street Journal*). (Perhaps Murdoch should have ditched his U.S. nationality and become an Italian?)[1]

This dust-up, which was barely covered on this side of the Atlantic, was suggestive of the complicated relationship between the European Union—spearheaded by Germany—whose combined markets and populations are larger than that of the U.S. and increasingly set the pace for the capitalist world generally, and U.S. imperialism, whose nationalist ego finds it difficult to accept that it is not the "indispensable nation" it purports to be.

U.S. imperialism also cannot bear to acknowledge that just as its hysterical anti-Sovietism of the Cold War led to the building up of both China and so-called "Islamic fundamentalism," a similar process led to the now muscular E.U., as a bulwark against Moscow. For the problem faced by U.S. imperialism after the landmark that was October 1917 is that Russia—even today—remains the pre-eminent European giant, with a population approaching 150 million, almost twice as much as the second largest nation: Germany. By way of contrast, Britain and France are about 60 million each. Besides, the size of Russia's territory dwarfs that administered by Berlin, Paris and London. Moreover, Russia contains a fabulous storehouse of natural resources, including oil and natural gas, sufficient to determine if Europeans are forced to freeze to death in the dark during a cold winter. Today in the cold light of history, it is not hard to see that irrespective of who rules in Moscow—even a capital friendly Vladimir Putin—Russia will have a prickly problem with U.S. imperialism, since this land bridge between Europe and Asia, this giant of the richest continent with the most extensive global holdings, has to be subverted if Washington is to bestride the planet like a colossus. Hence, during the Soviet era, a consolidated Europe, thought some of the brightest minds in Washington, could stand as a bulwark against Moscow.

But now the Soviet era has ended—at least for the time being—and U.S. imperialism is faced with a European juggernaut with a population of 500 million (and even without further expansion still easily tops U.S. imperialism's comparatively puny 300 million) and ideas of global hegemony of its own. Moreover, Europe contains influential Socialist and Communist parties, with deep roots in their respective nations and a healthy contempt for U.S. imperialism.

Even Washington's fellow imperialists across the ocean have reason to look askance at U.S. imperialism. There are those in London—and especially Paris—who recall with rancor the Suez War of 1956 when Washington felt compelled to go against its erstwhile allies and warn these powers (which at the time were joined by Israel) to stand down from its joint attack on the anti-imperialist action of Egypt's G.A. Nasser, who only recently had seized what was rightfully his nation's: the Suez Canal. Stung to the quick, London chose to calibrate its actions more carefully with those of Washington to prevent such a fiasco from recurring, while Paris decided that it should operate more independently from U.S. imperialism—which would come to include a partial withdrawal from the anti-Soviet bastion only recently established: NATO, i.e. the North Atlantic Treaty Organization. (Strikingly, with London blaming the "cowboy capitalism" of a deregulated U.S. for helping to spur runs on banks in episodes not seen in the UK since the 1860s, and pulling back its troops from Basra, Iraq, the fabled Anglo-American "special relationship" may be cooling, while the conservative French regime of Nicholas Sarkozy may be warming up to Washington, as suggested by everything from his anti-Iran rhetoric to vacationing down the road from the Bush summer home in Maine).

As many Europeans see it, U.S. imperialism—with its pro-death penalty hysteria, its antediluvian religiosity, its violence-soaked gun culture, its toxic contempt for sane environmental measures, its deep-seated political conservatism—has become a major threat to human existence. The war in Afghanistan, where Europeans were snookered into taking on a combat role so that Washington could then move on to tackle Iraq in a desperate gambit to control the global oil supply and thereby place their tightening palm on the windpipe of their competitors' economies, has only served to exacerbate this antipathy to US imperialism. The war in Iraq has been particularly worrisome to Brussels since Europe is closer to this now volatile region and contains restive Muslim populations that are not pleased with their governments' collaboration with the perceived Islamphobia that is now seen as animating the foreign policy of U.S. imperialism.

Yet even before these transforming conflicts in Iraq and Afghanistan, evidence was rampant that the blunders and missteps of the Bush regime had led to a plummeting of US-EU relations to an all-time low. When Bush the Lesser landed in Spain in June 2001 to begin a five-day European tour, he immediately faced stormy criticism of his policies on missile defense, global warming and capital punishment, voiced by government leaders and street demonstrators alike.[2] Part of the problem is that as the tip of the imperialist spear during the Cold War, the U.S. was compelled to move further to the right than its erstwhile European allies. An unhealthy contempt for the very concept of government—fueled by Washington's role in nullifying property in enslaved Africans without compensation, as the Civil War concluded—had metastasized into a core notion of U.S. conservatives. Meanwhile, even the British—supposedly closer ideologically to Washington—would be unwilling to relinquish their "socialized medicine" for the "free market" dominated counterpart across the Atlantic.

Hence, even before the turning point that was 11 September 2001, Europeans—en masse—had soured on the Bush regime. Thus, on 15 August of that fateful year, the *New York Times* reported that "ordinary Europeans strongly back their political leaders' unhappiness with American foreign policy on specific issues like the Kyoto environmental treaty and the Bush administration's threat to withdraw from the 1972 Anti-Ballistic Missile treaty....." A whopping 73% of those polled said Bush made decisions "entirely on U.S. interests" without considering European interests; a startling 79% of British and 85% of French shared this view.

Of course, there is a material basis for the growing European contempt for U.S. imperialism—which has soared beyond the ranks of the left and working class movement. The *Financial Times*, the voice of EU elites, whose excoriation of U.S. imperialism often exceeds the screeds of the U.S. left, is exemplary. It frequently expresses schadenfreude at the relative decline of U.S. imperialism. "Europe's economy is growing faster than the U.S.," it chortled in the Spring of 2007, well before the financial meltdown of August that sent the dollar on a nosedive. "The euro has gained against the dollar for all of this century;" while "Germany out-performed all other big markets in the first quarter, " the U.S. "S&P was flat." [3]

The inter-imperialist rivalry between the U.S. and E.U. has become ever sharper as a result, with the two mastodons jousting over markets world-wide. In 2001 Chiquita Brands actually sued the E.U. for a half-billion dollars (given this currency's precipitous drop, they may want to sue in euros). Based in Cincinnati, this company which is accustomed to having its way in Colombia and other hemispheric markets, contends that E.U. trade barriers have contributed directly to the financial difficulties that had forced Chiquita to suspend payment on its debts and pushed it to the brink of bankruptcy.[4] The monopoly that is Microsoft flummoxed and outfoxed antitrust regulators in Washington—before being humbled by Brussels in September 2007, a defeat that whetted the European appetite for further assaults on Apple and Intel. This major setback was seen in Redmond, Washington, as just another blatant and cynical attempt by European competitors to batter yet another U.S. interest.[5] Neelie Kroes, the EU competition commissioner firmly rebuffed U.S. criticism of Brussels' judgment after a number of U.S. lawmakers and a Justice Department official had questioned it. In unusually harsh terms, she asserted, "it is totally unacceptable that a representative of the U.S. administration criticized an independent court of law outside its jurisdiction. The European Commission," she added with bitterness, "does not pass judgment on rulings by U.S. courts and we expect the same degree of respect." [6] Of course, German's SAP and Linux, originally developed by a Scandinavian national, are bound to profit if Microsoft is restrained.

Microsoft's Seattle neighbor is similarly displeased with European efforts to clip their wings. Boeing, a major Pentagon contractor, has been subjected to a steady and repetitive drumfire from its European competitor, Airbus. The latest fusillade was launched in the Spring of 2007 when Airbus charged that Boeing is receiving massive subsidies from the U.S. government totaling a breathtaking $23.7 billion in breach of World Trade Organization rules. Airbus asserts that these "lavish" subventions have allowed Boeing to "engage in aggressive pricing of its aircraft which has caused lost sales, lost market share and price suppression to Airbus on a number of select markets." This is the biggest conflict ever handled by the WTO.[7]

This conflict is part of a battle in the skies that would startle even Flash Gordon. Brussels and Washington have been negotiating for the longest a so-called "open skies" compact regulating which of their airlines can dominate the lucrative trans-Atlantic market. The *Financial Times* was not alone in castigating this pact as "lopsided" since it gave "U.S. operators the right to fly between EU member states, while their own domestic markets remained closed." Sir Richard Branson of London, the publicity-hungry billionaire who has the ear of whomever happens to occupy 10 Downing Street, was unhappy when his Virgin America was blocked from flying into and out of U.S. airports [8] — which was guaranteed to complicate the already complex relations between Whitehall and Foggy Bottom.

But these celestial scrapes are minor compared to what lies on the horizon. Brussels has pledged to press ahead with plans to develop a satellite navigation system with the explicit aim of providing "independence" from the U.S. This is actually part of a battle for the skies that could easily spin out of control, since China is building its Beidou and Russia is improving its Glonass system.[9]

It is no secret that satellites are essential to military operations — and not only command, control and communications, the mantra of contemporary warfare — and U.S. imperialism has become concerned that the EU may want to supplement its growing economic strength with a military component: thus, the importance Washington places on NATO and domination of it by the U.S. Hence, U.S. imperialism has grave misgivings about the "European Security and Defense Initiative" and other efforts to develop an independent military prowess.[10] In particular, such an initiative could serve to erode the huge market share in global military sales now enjoyed by the likes of Boeing, Northrop Grumman and other merchants of death.

The WTO is becoming an arena for ever more savage battles between Brussels and Washington. After the WTO — at Brussels' behest — ruled that a $100 billion corporate tax break was an illegal trade subsidy, the howls of outrage ricocheted across the Atlantic. Graciously, Brussels chose to give Washington time to change its law — then threatened to impose harsh new tariffs on California raisins and Florida citrus, with the obvious aim of influencing voters that were marching to the polls in the then forthcoming and crucial November 2002 elections.[11]

The battles on the ground between Brussels and Washington are becoming increasingly riddled with conflict. These conflicts over domination of markets has spilled over into ordinary diplomacy making it difficult for the leading imperialist powers to maintain a consolidated line against up and coming rivals. Such is the case with regard to Iran, where the "EU 3" — Britain, France and Germany — took the lead in seeking to settle the dispute over Teheran's development of civilian nuclear energy. Given U.S. imperialism's unashamed and barefaced attempt to gain a stranglehold on global oil supplies by seizing Iraq, Brussels has been skeptical of Washington's jingoism — though it too would like to keep Iran in check. Germany, one of Iran's top trading partners, has quite a bit to lose as negotiations proceed. Berlin is concerned that — as has been its wont—Washington will seek to apply U.S. law beyond its shores in order to handicap its rivals.[12]

This suspicion of the deeper motives of U.S. imperialism has hampered the so-called "war against terror." It is not just the wariness about Washington's open hunger for domination of the market in petroleum, it is also the fact that conservative hawks in the U.S. have expressed such undisguised contempt for the niceties of civil liberties—which does not go down very well in Europe. This is what underlies the unusual Italian indictment of 26 U.S. nationals—many of them intelligence agents—in connection with the case of an Egyptian cleric, Hassan Mustafa Osama Nasr, who disappeared near his mosque in Milan in early 2003—apparently kidnapped by the U.S. authorities. As *The New York Times* delicately put it, "the indictment marked a turning point in Europe, where anger is high at the American program of 'extraordinary renditions,' an aggressive policy of seizing suspected terrorists on foreign soil and interrogating them at secret locations in a third country." [13] The unfortunate cleric may have wound up at a secret U.S. administered compound in Poland where it was revealed that interrogations were held. Brussels was incensed—it would be as if the EU were interrogating prisoners in Louisiana without informing the U.S. Others recognized the peril of admitting an anticommunist ally of U.S. imperialism like Poland into the EU.[14]

Italy, historically the home to one of the strongest left movements on the continent, is also in an uproar over proposals to make Vicenza the largest U.S. military site in Europe. In February 2007 over 200,000 marched in protest there. Code Pink, the U.S.-based feminist activist grouping, launched a petition website where they are collecting signatures of U.S. nationals in support of the besieged people of Vicenza.[15]

Before this dispute, members of the European Parliament who were investigating the ultra-secretive global eavesdropper, the U.S.-based National Security Agency, left in anger and disgust when members of the Bush regime refused to meet with them. Code-named "Echelon," this NSA program is a metaphor for what France routinely denounces as "Anglo-Saxon" hegemony in that Washington's partners in intercepting within Europe all email, telephone and fax communications are Britain, Australia, Canada and New Zealand. "Economic espionage" is reputedly a key objective for this cabal.[16] Many Germans cannot understand why U.S. imperialism has 12,000 intelligence agents on their soil—though the Soviet Union, the ostensible cause for their presence, has passed into history. Others know that part of their purpose is "economic espionage," which has proven critical—e.g. in 1994 when Saudi Arabia inked a deal with Boeing instead of Airbus after U.S. intelligence agents passed along confidential, proprietary information from the Seattle giant's chief competitor.[17] This utter disregard by U.S. imperialism of the sovereignty of major powers is quite worrying in Europe, suggesting that Washington feels it can treat the entire globe as its backyard.

The problem for the EU—at least according to some in Brussels—is that even if it stands tall against U.S. imperialism, this provides no answer for a rising China and India, whose populations are far more than twice as large and who do not carry the heavy baggage in Africa, Asia and Latin America as those who previously trumpeted the alleged virtues of white supremacy. Perhaps sensing this dilemma, Germany's Angela Merkel has bruited the idea of an enhanced "transatlantic partnership" that would bring U.S. imperialism and EU imperialism closer together. The outstanding question is if the yawning gulf between the two can be bridged as long as conservatism retains influence on this side of the Atlantic, while Socialist and Communist parties do the same in Europe: related to this is whether Europeans of various classes can be made to submerge their considerable hostility toward "cowboy capitalism" in the interest of imperialist unity.[18]

But even if Brussels and Washington can set aside their considerable differences, a specter still haunts the old continent: and that is Russia. The Soviet Union was dissolved, the Communist Party was ousted—yet relations between Moscow and what is euphemistically referred to as "the West" remain exceedingly complicated and often contentious. It is only natural that the largest and most populous nation on the continent would exercise wide influence but, evidently, this reality is difficult for some to accept.

Berlin is hedging, in any event. Social Democratic leader and former Chancellor, Gerhard Schroeder, raised eyebrows when he signed a lucrative contract with the massive Russian energy giant, Gazprom, upon leaving office. His successor, Angela Merkel (a fluent Russian speaker, just as Vladimir Putin speaks German fluently), has not broken with the deeply rooted German policy of entente with Russia, since hostility to Moscow was the cause for gargantuan disasters for Berlin—even before the 20th century. These relations have proceeded to the point that in the Spring of 2006 M.K. Bhardrakumar, India's former Ambassador to both Turkey and Uzbekistan, detected the "lengthening shadows of the Russian-German ties across the vast landscape of Central and Eastern Europe and Eurasia (and even stretching all the way to China) that are steadily, inexorably reconfiguring the international system." [19]

U.S. imperialism's attempt to woo Germany were not helped when news emerged that Washington planned to "punish German 'treachery'" after Berlin chose not to back what turned out to be an illegal and criminal invasion and occupation of Iraq. Germans of various classes and ideological persuasions had to be concerned about a U.S. imperialism that is increasingly intoxicated from the fumes emitted by its own self-praise.[20] But as U.S. imperialism saw it, this was nothing more than appropriate payback. For didn't France block the appointment of a U.S. national to a high-level UN appointment, overseeing peacekeeping?

As in Western Europe, revulsion toward U.S. imperialism has escalated in Moscow. The unseemly dancing on the grave of the Soviet Union, the backing of the looting of natural resources, and virtual glee at Russian impoverishment, have soured millions of Russians toward Washington. Even the newly minted oligarchs of Moscow, logical allies of U.S. imperialism, have their doubts and criticisms. Recall the events of early 2000, not long after Putin's ascension, when the Export-Import Bank of Washington succumbed to pressure from U.S. monopoly interests to refuse a loan guarantee to Tyumen Oil Co. of Russia to exploit Russian oilfields. Objecting to the loan guarantee were BP Amoco, financier George Soros and the powerhouse lobbying firm, Patton Boggs. Unusually, BP Amoco was allowed to submit a document that it had commissioned—though it had been prepared by the CIA and stamped "Secret"—to sink the deal. Now those familiar with the ordinary corruption of state monopoly capitalism were not surprised when a private firm enlisted a government agency on its behalf—but for many Russians who had swallowed the Kool-Aid about the sweetness and light that supposedly inhered in alleged "free markets" were outraged. Clawing back control over Russian resources from the clutches of the likes of BP Amoco was one of Putin's top priorities—and a source of grand hostility toward him by U.S. imperialism.[22]

Ordinary Russians were terribly upset when word leaked that a U.S. envoy had met with Chechen rebels who had just murdered 21 of their compatriots and wounded 130 in bomb attacks.[23] This was before the tragedy of 11 September, when the tie between Chechen rebels and Al Qaeda was then revealed.

The arrogance of U.S. imperialism, punch-drunk as it is from repeated global confrontations with opponents worthy and not, has made it difficult for Washington to recognize how isolated it has become. This attempt to court India is bound to end badly, not only because New Delhi has little interest in encircling China on Washington's behalf but also because New Delhi and Moscow were allies, even during the darkest days of the Cold War—and are determined to remain so. Thus, in October 2000 President Putin turned up in New Delhi where the two sides agreed "to build a multipolar global structure"—code for repudiation of Washington's unilateralism.[24] Actually, since the U.S. has moved so far to the right, if anything it is likely that India will align itself with Russia and

China, which are more ideologically compatible with a nation that has two influential Communist parties.

There is little doubt that Russia and China have attained a degree of closeness that is formidable. Particularly since the Kosovo conflict in the Spring of 1999, Moscow and Beijing have engaged in joint military training, sharing of data on the formulation of military doctrine—and the blossoming of what amounts to a military alliance. Thousands of Russian personnel are working at Chinese research institutes on such matters as laser technology, the miniaturization of nuclear weapons; cruise missiles; space-based weaponry; and nuclear submarines. In a historic departure, the Russian-built Sovremenny-class destroyer Hangzhou left St. Petersburg on 4 January 2000 with a mixed crew of Chinese and Russian sailors. The vessel has become the largest warship in the Chinese navy, equipped with sophisticated Sunburn missiles. In 1992 China bought its first batch of Su-27 fighter jets from Russia. If U.S. imperialism and Beijing collide in the Taiwan Straits, China will be prepared—thanks to Russia.[25] Stephen Blank of the U.S.-based Army War College recognized this when he warned against China's "anti-American" alliance with Russia, and argued in the Summer of 2000 that a fight over Taiwan would also mean active participation by Moscow.[26] "Sino-Russian relations are enjoying their best period ever," beamed Chinese Premier Zhu Rongji in the Fall of 2000—and, if anything, he was downplaying developments.[27]

Conflict between Beijing and Moscow, which was essential to the collapse of the Soviet Union, has been reversed with consequences of enormous magnitude for the fate of U.S. imperialism.

The heightened relations between Beijing and Moscow were exemplified further when in early 2001 they negotiated their first political treaty since the heady days following the triumph of the Chinese Revolution in 1949. This pact marked the first time that China had entered into a political accord in decades, reinforcing the unique nature of their bilateral relations. This was said to be prompted by the Bush regime's emphasis on anti-missile defense, seen as code for a nuclear first strike on the emerging EuroAsian bloc.[28]

Recent events have indicated that there has been no surcease in the growing ties between Russia and China, which, combined with Washington's growing alienation from Brussels, open up the possibility of a massive global shift to the left, reversing the early results of the collapse of the Soviet Union. It was during the Summer of 2005 that Russia and China held their first ever joint military exercises—this after Uzbekistan gave U.S. forces 180 days to depart from their base there, sensing that they realized which way the winds are blowing. "We are facing the same threat," said Ni Lexiong ominously: this well-connected military expert teaches at Shanghai Normal University.[29]

President Hu Jintao of China and President Putin meet so frequently nowadays that their summits—arguably the most important bilateral
relationship in the world today—are hardly considered news. Thus in the
Spring of 2007, there they were again, clinking glasses in Moscow and
signing agreements on trade and the economy, including several banking
deals; cooperation on exploration of Mars; increased oil shipments to
China; and expanded relations in such sensitive realms as aerospace, bio-
engineering and information technology.[30]

U.S. imperialism has become increasingly worried about Moscow's
orientation. As Washington sees it, Russia has turned away from "the
West" or being a U.S. flunky, toward a role that provides it with more
global muscle. This has led to the release of a remarkable document,
released by the elite Manhattan-based Council on Foreign Relations, complaining of "Russia's Wrong Direction." Co-authored by Republican Jack
Kemp and Democrat John Edwards, it was accompanied by an equally
remarkable news account that suggested that Washington was seeking
"regime change" in Moscow, a new Cold War, the formation of "anti-
Moscow military alliances" (as if NATO were not enough) and providing
"overt support" to Putin's opponents (perhaps Putin should return the
favor and provide "overt support" to opponents of the Bush regime).[31]

While U.S. imperialism continues to celebrate with ecstasy the fall
of the Soviet Union, Russia has built up a huge cache of foreign currency
reserves, repaid debts ahead of schedule and increased its global profile.
Moscow still controls a huge amount of territory, enormous natural
resources, space technology, scientific expertise, atomic technology, a
sizeable defense industry, a permanent seat on the UN Security Council—
and more. It controls 20% of the world's natural gas reserves (and lately
Putin has been trying to work with Algeria—Europe's other chief supplier—in forming a gas equivalent of OPEC). Though it is a major supplier
to Europe, this resource could just as easily be re-routed to China and/or
India—and this would be of titanic geo-economic significance. Thus, the
Indian political leader, M.K. Bhardrakumar, was not far wrong, when he
concluded that "Russia is turning out to be one of the biggest beneficiar-
ies of the phenomenon of globalization in the post-Soviet era. The 'victor'
[or 'the West'] ending up as a dependent of the 'vanquished' [i.e.
Russia]—is a rare occurrence in history. It creates profound psychological
problems. It can be the stuff of cold wars." [32] How true. But Washington
has made a habit of prematurely proclaiming "mission accomplished" and
victory attained—as Bush the Lesser's May 2003 speech proclaiming both
in Iraq attested.

An emboldened Putin, sensing the historical turnabout, seems to almost take unalloyed glee in making evident what has yet to be grasped on this side of the Atlantic—a tectonic shift is occurring in the global correlation of forces, and this is operating to the disadvantage of the self-proclaimed "sole remaining superpower." In June 2007, the Russian leader said the world needed to create a new international financial architecture to replace the "archaic, undemocratic and unwieldy" existing model. This was necessary, he said, since 60% of global GDP comes from beyond the confines of the Group of Seven, led by U.S. imperialism. This was a few days after he had warned that Russia might target nuclear missiles at Europe if the U.S. built a missile shield in Poland and the Czech Republic.[33] And prior to that, Putin announced that he would suspend its compliance with a treaty on conventional arms in Europe—again in response to anti-missile defense plans. Further, Putin has pledged to strengthen Russia's military and step up espionage targeting NATO nations, in response to the aggressive plans of U.S. imperialism.[34]

In a—perhaps—unrelated maneuver, the Russian space agency has announced plans to launch eight navigation satellites by December 2007—in direct competition with the U.S.'s Global Positioning System.[35]

Suggestive of the mass global unpopularity of U.S. imperialism is the fact that Putin's maneuvers have been hailed widely. The *Lebanese Daily Star* noted that a visit to Moscow by the Egyptian leadership in order to increase defense ties and sign large arms deals would be heard loudly in Washington in the first place.[36] "Russia Stages a Comeback Through Syria" was their headline of 28 August 2006. Hailed was the welcoming of a Hamas delegation to Moscow and Russia's involvement in modernizing Syrian port facilities. Like millions elsewhere, whatever sympathies that many Lebanese may have held in favor of the former Soviet Union, it was well recognized that its collapse warped global politics, strengthening conservative hawks in Washington who then made a desperate grab to control world oil supplies, to the detriment of Arabs in the first place. Now reality itself was sobering these adventurers and a rising Russia was no small reason. The *Teheran Times* put it bluntly, cheering for a restoration of the "international status Moscow enjoyed during the Cold War," which was needed to "counter U.S. influence." [37] Writing for South Africa's *Mail & Guardian* on 18 April 2007, one commentator was so bold as to pronounce that "the era of U.S. hegemony is now over."

Unwilling to accept gracefully its relative decline, U.S. imperialism is now gambling on what it sees as its trump card—the military—though one would have thought that Iraq had exposed the folly of such a pursuit. No matter. The Bush regime is determined to install anti-missile shields in Europe, supposedly to block Iranian missiles (though Putin asked wondrously, why not place such gimmickry in, say, Azerbaijan?) But in the early days of Bush's tenure, the *South China Morning Post* exposed the reality—this son of Star Wars was designed to "contain China and Russia."[38] Others suggested that this plan was little more than a cover for the unthinkable—a nuclear first strike against Russia and China with no fear of retaliation because of a hardened anti-missile shield.

The distinguished biographer of economist John Maynard Keynes, Robert Skidelsky, who now sits in the House of Lords in London, argued that the purpose of this Bush scheme "is to neutralize Russia's nuclear capability. Russia would be deprived of the ability to deter an American attack whether nuclear or conventional." This was no more than "American military unilateralism."[39]

Sensing that they may have bet on a losing horse, the vast majority of the population of the Czech Republic have opposed the idea of their nation hosting a so-called shield—that may not even work but will place it in the crossfire of a possible nuclear strike and counter-strike.[40] They are emulating the EU's top diplomat, Javier Solana of Spain, who as early as May 2000 warned that this cockeyed plan would alarm NATO.[41] According to the *Financial Times*, "Many Poles feel their country got almost nothing for swiftly agreeing to help out in Iraq and are now wary of getting entangled in another Bush administration proposal."[42] Even the ultra-right League of Polish Families and the demagogically populist Self-Defense Party are skeptical of the missile shield. In response, congressional critics in Washington and peace activists nationally have stressed that the Bush regime has already spent more than four years and billions of dollars building a similar system based in Alaska and Central California aimed at shooting down missiles from North Korea—a system that has proved highly erratic in testing. So moved, the House of Representatives cut the White House's funding request for shields by half and barred the Pentagon from starting construction. The Senate acted similarly in June 2007.[43] It seemed that increasing numbers were coming to see that the shield—besides being an unworkable form of intimidation—was little more than a naked attempt to again transfer taxpayer dollars into the pockets of the merchants of death.

Growing numbers on this side of the Atlantic realize that the combative and confrontational Bush regime are pushing the planet to the brink of an unimaginable conflict that would push humanity closer to extinction faster than his equally insane non-plans to deal with climate change. So prompted, Moscow has joined with Beijing in knocking together the Shanghai Cooperation Organization, a kind of Eur-Asian version of the old Warsaw Pact. In August 2007 the Iranian leadership attended their summit, which was more than a veiled warning to U.S. imperialism.[44] Moscow continues to have influence on the "Northern Alliance" of

Afghanistan and has made overtures to EU nations now bogged down in that nation about settling this conflict with the Taliban. This too could nudge U.S. imperialism from its alleged pre-eminence. Again, M.K. Bhadrakumar summed things up succinctly when he said, "the U.S. will increasingly find itself under compulsion to perform as a team player, which suits neither its geo-strategy nor its standing as the [alleged] sole superpower." [45]

What may be deceiving U.S. imperialism is that it has established a substantial domination of non-Russian Eastern Europe, which feeds notions of Cold War triumph—but even this is being challenged by the European Union, which has swallowed Poland and is poised to masticate and digest Romania and Bulgaria. The EU is debating whether or not to accept Turkey, whose huge population would make it second only to Germany. Washington officially supports this accession but there is real doubt if U.S. imperialism would like to see the EU further strengthened. If the situation in Iraq continues to deteriorate and Iraqi Kurds seek independence, this could bring an intervention by Ankara and possibly destroy its EU chances, which anti-Muslim bias is blocking, in any case.

Washington performed yeoman service in whipping up so-called "Islamic fundamentalism" in the former Ottoman Empire of the Balkans, which contributed mightily to the breakup of Socialist Yugoslavia. It was on 11 March 2001 that the *London Observer* reported a story that should have made banner headlines in the U.S. but—typically—did not: "The United States secretly supported the ethnic Albanian [Muslim] extremists now behind insurgencies in Macedonia and southern Serbia," including the contested region of Kosovo, yet another point of dispute between Moscow and Washington, since the latter backs independence for this region and the former does not. But suggestive of how U.S. imperialism is driving the EU closer to Russia is the fact that Brussels, too, was upset: "European officers," it was said, "are furious that the Americans have allowed guerrilla armies ...to train, smuggle arms and launch attacks across two international borders." Beijing too was not happy with Washington's Balkans policy, as suggested the visit to Belgrade of the then second-ranking member of the ruling Communist Party, Li Peng, in June 2000. As the *South China Morning Post* put it, this was a "sign of support for President Slobodan Milosevic's government which is politically isolated by the United States and its allies." [46] The allegedly accidental bombing of the Chinese embassy in Belgrade by U.S. imperialist war planes—a scant year before this visit—was perceived widely as a signal to Beijing, akin to a punch in the nose, to steer clear of the Balkans: the upshot was to drive China closer to Russia.

The back story was that after Serbian military radio centers had been destroyed in initial airstrikes by the U.S. and its allies, Belgrade was said to have transferred operations to the Chinese embassy, in exchange for which the Chinese received the pieces of the F-117 that had been shot down earlier. The result? U.S. imperialism destroyed the Chinese embassy.[47]

Progressive forces in the U.S. tried valiantly to alert the public to U.S. imperialism's alliance with reactionaries in the Balkans. The writer, Conn Hallinan, pointed out how the U.S. "trained the Croats who ethnically cleansed 350,000 Croatian Serbs from Krajina Province in 1995" and how Washington's allies in Kosovo had "deep ties with the drug trade in Europe and North America."[48] Certainly, U.S. imperialism can be proud that it helped destroy socialism in Eastern Europe and opened up virgin territory for their capital flows. How this benefits the U.S. working class—some of whose organizations backed the foreign policy that led to increased competition from low-cost labor—is less clear. Thus, the New York billionaire cosmetics heir, Ronald Lauder, has reason to celebrate. Of course, he was accused of paying $1 million in bribes to Ukrainian officials for a valuable television license that formerly belonged to the state; this station complemented other stations he has picked up for a song in the region. He donated $100,000 to George Bush's 2001 inauguration, chairs the Board of the posh Museum of Modern Art in Manhattan, and served Ronald Reagan as his Ambassador to Austria, where he collected useful contacts that paid off in handsome investments. According to law enforcement officials, his partners in his TV ventures had close ties to organized crime elements—a force that has sprouted like mushrooms after a spring rain in post-Communist Eastern Europe.[49] Even if one was hostile to the previous regimes, it is difficult to argue that their successors represent a great leap forward.

Still, Philip Morris should be joyful also. The Czech Republic sold its state-owned tobacco industry to this U.S. monopoly of death, giving it domination of this deadly business. Perversely, this company argued that it was saving the state millions of dollars in social welfare payments and other costs as smokers were perishing prematurely. This was "hyena-ism" cried progressives, as Philip Morris raked in profits [50]—which should forever stand as a metaphor for the ravages brought to Europe in the wake of U.S. imperialism's triumph.

In the long run, however, what will tell is the widespread European hostility to U.S. imperialism. Polls suggest that Europeans have little faith that they can meet the challenge provided by a rising Asia—but are even more convinced that their continent and union should not become more like the U.S., whose reputation continues to plummet. This sentiment is most advanced in Italy,[51] whose Communist Party would have come to power in the late 1940s but for the blatant interference of Washington. The problem for U.S. imperialism is that even the CIA seems incapable of arresting its precipitous decline in prestige.

6: AFRICA ARISES

"Look East My son.....Look East"

Those were the sage words of Kenyan journalist, Wanjohi Kabukuru, as he assayed the results of his President's visit to Beijing, in just the latest journey from the continent — Africa — most ravaged by the savagery of imperialism and, ironically, where the crisis of U.S. imperialism has become most evident. For of late there has been a growing hysteria in Washington that China is stealing a march on U.S. imperialism, providing an alternative which means that Africa is not bound to bend the knee when their leaders cross the Atlantic. Naturally, U.S. imperialism has responded by upping the ante in the only category where it still thinks it rules: the military option.[1]

But Kenyans were not wracked with anxiety with this prospect when President Mwai Kibaki arrived in China in 2005. Instead, they were happy that he came home with multi-million dollar loans and grants for improvements of Nairobi's power distribution system. Kibaki also signed a contract with the Chinese technological giant, Huawei Technologies Company, to provide wireless telecoms to all government district offices and link them with the central government in Nairobi.

Kenyans are not the only Africans who are pleased with China's peaceful rise, for this Asian nation's trade with the continent as a whole has jumped dramatically, reaching approximately $35 billion in 2005 after growth rates of 50% in 2003 and 59% in 2004. Chinese entities have invested heavily in copper and cobalt mines in the Democratic Republic of the Congo, including building roads. It is helping Ethiopia build the continent's biggest dam; it has helped Nigeria launch a communications satellite, and introduced a new anti-malarial drug in Uganda.[2]

China's economic engagement with Africa is breathtaking and, quite frankly, may be the beginning of the end of a destructive cycle for the beset continent, inaugurated by the unlamented Slave Trade, which developed Europe and North America as it undeveloped Africa. Now, appropriately, Africa is beginning to recover, as U.S. imperialism enters an era of profound crisis. In the Spring of 2007 — to cite one example among many — Beijing pledged to provide about $20 billion in infrastructure and trade financing to Africa during the next three years, eclipsing many of the continent's big donors in a single pledge. These big donors—dominated by the North Atlantic powers—had pledged about $7 billion via multi-lateral agencies, according to Donald Kaberuka, President of the African Development Bank. Yes, grants and soft loans from these donors to Africa from Europe, the U.S. and Japan still exceed China's, though they come with conditions attached, and often fail to materialize when these conditions are not met.[3]

The new day for a New Africa was on display naturally, in Beijing in the late Fall of 2006. For it was then that all African nations were invited to a two-day summit. Even the five nations that recognize Taiwan and not Beijing as "China" were invited to send representatives.[4]

Beijing's policy towards the Congo is most revealing. For the past decade, millions have perished in this sprawling central African nation, the site for this planet's most destructive humanitarian catastrophe since the end of World War II. Congo, which was a former prime hunting ground for slave dealers who enhanced the wealth of Europe and North America, also had been ruled for decades by the dictatorial friend of Washington—Mobutu Sese Soko. Though elections have taken place that added needed legitimacy to the administration of President Joseph Kabila, the North Atlantic powers—while focusing intently on Zimbabwe, a nation in which most Congolese would be happy to reside—have been lethargic in assisting Congo. Thus, there was a combination of both alarm and unease on the part of these powers when Beijing announced in September 2007 that it planned to lend Congo a hefty $5 billion to modernize its decrepit infrastructure, including roads and railways, 31 hospitals, 145 health centers and two universities. And part of the loan will go into Congo's mining sector, a treasure trove that also includes gold and diamonds.[5] Instead of glee at the prospect that a besieged Congo was receiving desperately needed assistance, a churlish International Monetary Fund basically instructed this sovereign state to reject funds from China.[6]

Unfortunately, as the African-American activist professor, Clarence Lusane, pointed out, arms dealers from the U.S. armed both sides in this fratricidal Congolese conflict. Ultimately the forces backing Kabila—backed by Namibia, Angola and Zimbabwe—were able to defeat his opponents backed by Rwanda, Uganda and Burundi, who were favored by influential forces in Washington.[7]

The result? As Wamba Dia Wamba, the Congolese intellectual and political leader, noted in the Spring of 2001, "in less than three years, about 2 million have died. There aren't any good health services, in the war zone, particularly. Soldiers have been using violence on women, so you have quite a few who are victims of HIV. ....the conditions of life are very bad and the conditions of reproduction, in terms of food, also are not good. In fact a study has said that as m such as one sixth of the population has problems finding access to food." [8] The fearsome Ebola, monkey pox, vaginal fistula and other diseases and maladies of biblical proportion have taken hold. Though the competition is stiff, Congo—an early and persistent victim of both the Slave Trade and brutal colonialism—probably has suffered more in recent years than other nations on this planet, and the gross interference of global imperialism has played no small role in this process.

This is a point well worth pondering—particularly when one answers a call on a mobile phone. For tantalum, the refined extract of Columbite—or coltan for short—is a critical element in mobile phones. And the Congo supplies a significant percentage of the world's supply, produced by miners toiling in horrifying, even startling, conditions. [9]

The severe limitations of U.S. imperialism's policy toward Africa is revealed in its one-sided policy toward Zimbabwe. This small Southern Africa nation with a population of about 11 million witnessed the influx of thousands of settlers from the Pan-European world—including the U.S. itself—beginning in the 1890s (though a significant percentage arrived after World War II) where they seized the land and resources and imposed a cruel system of legalized racism. After a bloody war of liberation—which saw covert and overt aid from Washington to the racists—independence was attained, and then the nation suffered once more as it aided South Africans oust apartheid. During this period, Washington turned a blind eye toward the excesses of the ruling party led by President Robert Mugabe, since he was perceived to be pro-China and not pro-Soviet (unlike his leading domestic opponents). But now that the Soviet Union has collapsed, the news media of U.S. imperialism have demonized Mugabe in frankly racist terms to the point where one must wonder if what drives them is nervousness about Harare's attempt to claw back the ill-gotten gains of settler colonialists—a term that could describe easily the rulers of the U.S., whose ancestors, too, ousted the indigenous. [10]

Yet, ironically, as China has stepped into the vacuum in Zimbabwe created by sanctions imposed by U.S. imperialism and its sidekick in London, few press accounts in the North Atlantic deign to note that Beijing's closeness to this regime was propelled in no small part by U.S. imperialism's anti-Sovietism. For the fact is—in a historic turnabout—Chinese entities have emerged as the dominant force in Zimbabwe's economy, which still retains a decent infrastructure of roads, and an educated populace. [11] On the other hand, after Harare expropriated the land of farmers from the European minority, Washington responded with bi-partisan sanctions endorsed by solons from Jesse Helms to Hillary Clinton and Russ Feingold.[12] Interestingly, though the North Atlantic powers—principally Washington and London—have been vitriolic in their denunciation of Harare, African nations (particularly Zimbabwe's neighbors) have been just as vehement in denouncing this approach (so much for the slogan du jour: "African Solutions for African problems"). For Zimbabwe's neighbors—notably South Africa and Namibia—still await a reckoning of their own as to how to confront the detritus of the bad old days of European settler colonialism.

Similarly, Asia and Latin America—notably Socialist Cuba—have been hostile to sanctions against Harare. Intriguingly, as recently as 1998 China ranked only 11th in Harare's roll call of importers—an indicator of how quickly change has occurred. Yet today informed estimates suggest that there are at least 15 sizeable Zimbabwe-China business deals, mostly involving state enterprises.[13]

Besides the fate of the European minority, Zimbabwe's wealth of resources—which includes gold, platinum, coal, nickel, diamonds, and the like—guarantees the continuing interest of U.S. imperialism and its allies. These resources—particularly petroleum—also guarantees that Africa as a whole will be of interest to U.S. imperialism. By 2005 this continent provided more oil to the U.S. than the Middle East. Three of the top 10 suppliers to the U.S. by 2005 were African—Nigeria, Algeria and Angola. Yet, here again the crisis of U.S. imperialism is no better revealed, for hands were wringing throughout Washington when in January 2006 China's state-run oil firm announced it would pay $2.3 billion for a 45% stake in a bountiful Nigerian oilfield; In May of that year President Hu Jintao made a triumphal visit to West Africa.[14]

Because of its lengthy history of anti-African racism and brutal exploitation of the continent—not to mention its hostility to the idea of a state sector at the commanding heights of the economy, which will be Africa's savior—U.S. imperialism is at a distinct disadvantage when it comes to competing with China. Angola has overtaken Saudi Arabia as China's premier supplier of crude oil and China is Luanda's second largest consumer of oil—behind the U.S. In March 2006 a new consortium was unveiled, Sonangol-Sinopec International, an enterprise jointly controlled by the state-owned oil company of Angola and China's Sinopec. Chinese companies have been at the forefront of Angola's reconstruction bonanza. A new airport is being built at Viana, just outside the capital, Luanda, one-third financed by the government, the rest by Chinese interests. At the time of Angola's independence from Portuguese colonialism in 1975, U.S. imperialism, Maoist China and apartheid South Africa shared the same trench in their opposition to the ultimate winning and still ruling MPLA

Party in Luanda, which was backed by Moscow and Havana. But today there is a new situation and if Angola is any indication, emerging from the rubble of the Cold War is a formidable China, now rebuilding in a $300 million deal the war-damaged Benguela railway, which stretches from the Democratic Republic of the Congo to the coast. Chinese loans have allowed Angola to forego funding from the International Monetary Fund—yet another blow to the pretensions of U.S. imperialism.[15]

Though Beijing rather rapidly backed away from its unsavory tie-up with apartheid South Africa, U.S. imperialism—which was marinated in white supremacy—has been less reluctant. In the early days of the Bush regime in 2001, his senior African official was in close touch with Angola's discredited UNITA rebels, despite UN sanctions banning contact with their representatives. Suggestive of the priorities of the Texas oil man, these contacts began the week after his inauguration. Interestingly, Karl Rove—"Bush's Brain"—was apparently behind this initiative.[16]

Within the next decade, recently discovered offshore reserves are expected to enable West Africa to out-produce the North Sea's oil rigs and capture even more of U.S. imperialism's oil-import market. This includes not just Nigeria and Angola (both once the site of slave hunting that populated North America) but also Chad (adjacent, not coincidentally, to Darfur, Sudan, another frequent topic of discussion in the U.S. media), whose oil will be shipped via Cameroon and Equatorial Guinea.[17]

Oil has fueled U.S. imperialism but the question Washington must face now is that world oilfields are only just meeting demand and are being drained faster than new production can be brought on line. And this is occurring as China presents an ever more stiff challenge to the hegemony of U.S. imperialism. This provides African nations with a more than viable alternative, and makes them less prone to docilely accept the routine bullying of Washington. Thus in the run-up to the disastrous March 2003 invasion of Iraq, Washington was seeking desperately to gain about ten votes on the all-important U.N. Security Council to add legitimacy to its brigandage. The key was Africa, notably Guinea, Cameroon and Angola. Washington-Paris relations reached a new low when France sent its top diplomats to these nations in order to lobby against a vote in favor of the war resolution. This was the backdrop for yet another wrinkle to U.S. imperialism's crisis—its troubled relation with Paris, which has pretensions of grandeur all its own, most of which are buoyed by its neo-colonial role in West Africa, now being challenged by Washington.

France is the major force in Guinea and Cameroon, for example, though Conakry's critically important bauxite is mostly bought by U.S. firms. More than 150 French companies and 20,000 French expatriates are in Cameroon. Unsurprisingly, Cameroon's long-time leader, Paul Biya—

whose depredations against his populace make Robert Mugabe look like Martin Luther King, Jr.—backed Paris' anti-invasion posture, a marker of what was to come: the U.S. did not get UN legitimacy for its war. Furthermore, Cameroon is at odds with its more powerful neighbor, Nigeria, over control of the oil-rich island of Bakassi.[18] France's colossal oil giant, Total, faces a decline of oil production in its traditional preserves—Gabon and Congo-Brazzaville—though in the latter nation there has been a recent major offshore discovery.[19] One major issue that anti-imperialists globally must ascertain is whether the inter-imperialist contradictions between Paris and Washington will be curbed by the ascension of President Nicholas Sarkozy's crude pro-Yankee tendencies.

As of this writing, it is not easy to draw conclusions. Paris' recent bloody intervention in the former Ivory Coast was so heavy-handed that some Africans wistfully wished for a rescue from U.S. imperialism! Paris still maintains troops in or about such hotspots as Chad, Central African Republic and Gabon, while being accused of stirring up ethnic tensions in Burundi and Rwanda—France was actually accused of fomenting genocide in the latter strife-torn nation.[20]

Nonetheless, the relative decline of U.S. imperialism—the locomotive of world imperialism—may be so significant that it will be unable to arrest the rising of Africa in league with China. This may have been exposed inferentially in the aftermath of the 2007 meeting in Germany of the leading industrial powers led by U.S. imperialism—the so-called G8 (which recently acceded to the admission of Russia to its hallowed ranks but still excludes China and India, the emerging dominant powers). Like the 2005 G8 summit in Gleneagles, Scotland, Africa was supposedly a top priority but the actual results suggest that global imperialism is unable to adapt to the challenge presented by China. The leading Canadian diplomat, Stephen Lewis, termed their initiatives on Africa as "intellectually dishonest and riddled with arithmetic sleight-of-hand." His scorn rising to indignation, he added, "the betrayal of Africa is almost a matter of principle for the G8." He was irate since their vows to adhere to the internationally agreed upon "Millennium Development Goals" designed to attack poverty and disease were clearly inadequate. The North Atlantic powers in particular, he charged, were "spending at least $120 billion each year to fight the wars in Iraq and Afghanistan," yet "the same countries can't even guarantee a paltry total of $60 billion over an unknown number of years to fight a pandemic [HIV-AIDS] that has taken 25 million lives and has 40 million people in its grip. I keep asking," he added mournfully, "what has happened to the world's moral anchor." Moreover, he concluded, "nowhere—and this is frankly astonishing—nowhere is there mention of the prospective international agency for women actively under discussion at the United Nations, as a vehicle to make a significant dent on the pandemic. Why?" [21]

Why indeed. U.S. imperialism and British neo-colonialism, who owe their present elevated status to the plunder of Africa, should be in the forefront of aiding the rise of this continent; instead, they abdicate their responsibility in favor of wars in Iraq and Afghanistan—and therefore create a huge opening for China to ride to the rescue.

Of course, given the importance of African oil, it would be a mistake to assume that U.S. imperialism has ruled out the possibility of military intervention in Africa itself—though one could easily imagine that the presence in their ranks of African-Americans may give Washington pause.

Actually, in May 2003 the ostentatiously titled "Supreme Commander" of NATO, General James Jones, indicated that in the future, U.S. naval forces would spend much less time in the Mediterranean Sea. Instead, he predicted, "I will bet they will spend half the time going down the west coast of Africa." Truth be told, this was nothing new. In the period preceding the U.S. Civil War, the U.S. naval forces were frequently to be found sailing down the west coast of Africa, supposedly in search of U.S. slave ships which were stealing human capital to deploy on plantations in Cuba and Brazil often controlled by U.S. nationals. [22] Historically, U.S. imperialism has derived its lifeblood from Africa and as this continent seeks to throw off its neo-colonial shackles—assisted by China—Washington responds in the only language it seems to understand: the logic of the gunboat.

Thus, in July 2004 the U.S. military carried out "Summer Pulse 04," a naval exercise that encompassed the globe but was designed to show capability in Africa notably. This was displayed off the coast of Morocco where the aircraft carrier USS Enterprise commanded a U.S. carrier battle group that led a massive joint exercise with naval forces from nine nations, including NATO nations and Morocco itself. Involved were 20,000 personnel (both sailors and marines) on board 30 ships. In October 2004, the U.S. European Command (EURCOM) hosted a three day Gulf of Guinea maritime security conference in Naples, Italy (headquarters of the notorious U.S. Sixth Fleet). The Gulf happens to be a major site of oil deposits. This was followed by a January 2005 two-month deployment by the U.S. Navy in the Gulf of Guinea with critical participation by the USS Emory, carrying about 1400 sailors and marines. There was another Gulf of Guinea deployment in May-June 2005—followed by others since.

These exercise are significant in that they show the capability of U.S. imperialism to deploy in oil-rich Africa without using bases while able to carry out—if need be—air strikes, airborne assaults and the like. A senior Pentagon official did not seek to hide the fact that petroleum and natural gas laden Nigeria was a particular concern of his.[23]

In a maneuver that has been the seedbed of a string of coups, the Pentagon is now training thousands of African troops, including those from such nations as Algeria, Chad, Mali, Mauretania, Niger, Senegal, Nigeria, Morocco and Tunisia—where the military has not been inactive politically, in any case. The Pentagon is also assigning more military officers to U.S. embassies in the region, bolstering the gathering and sharing of intelligence, casing austere landing strips for use in "emergencies" and securing greater access and legal protections for U.S. troops through new bilateral agreements—just in case, these traditionally trigger-happy soldiers get, as is their wont, itchy fingers.[24]

Lest one think that East Africa—also the homeland for countless African-Americans—is being neglected, consider that one of the major deployments of U.S. troops is in Djibouti, traditionally a site of French influence, not far distant from Saudi Arabia. It was from Djibouti in November 2001 that CIA operatives directed the flight of the Predator drone aircraft that was used to fire the missiles that killed an alleged Al-Qaeda leader and four others in Yemen. Similarly, the U.S. maintains important military facilities at a base on the Indian Ocean island of Diego Garcia: the African nation of Mauritius continues to claim sovereignty here though in a cruel act of displacement, Britain (the former colonial power) compelled the indigenes to move elsewhere. U.S. imperialism uses the island to base a floating stockpile of tanks, armored vehicles, ammunition and other military hardware sufficient to equip an Army brigade of up to 3500 troops and a division of 17,300 Marines. The U.S. Air Force also bases B-52 and B-2 bombers at airfields on Diego Garcia. The facilities at Diego Garcia played a significant role in the Gulf War of 1991 and U.S. military operations in Afghanistan and Iraq subsequently. Complementing these assets is that Nairobi allows U.S. troops to use the strategic port of Mombasa, which came in handy during the 1992-1994 intervention in neighboring Somalia.[25]

The ostensible basis for this Pentagon descent upon Africa is the so-called "global war against terrorism," with the lust for petroleum not being deemed sufficiently respectable to highlight. Thus, a U.S. "anti-terror team" arrived in Mauretania in early 2004, then moved on to the Chad-Niger border. With U.S. military forces supplying satellite surveillance, Algerian, Malian and Nigerien forces pursued "terrorists" shortly thereafter. Thereafter the Sahara-Sahel region—a dusty mélange of mud-huts and barely navigable roads in the midst of a sprawling desert, spreading like an oil-spot, became a new front in the "war against terror." Yet, the man designated as Bin Laden's surrogate in the region was believed to have been trained as a Green Beret in Fort Bragg, North Carolina in the 1990s—not the first time that "blowback" has hit U.S. imperialism. As it turns out, this has not necessarily been a typical boomerang in that the "war against terror" neatly helps to justify petro-imperialism. Simultaneously, the militarizing of nations with fragile polities has served to propel the Tuareg revolts in Mali and Niger, a coup in Mauretania, riots in southern Algeria, political crisis in Chad and inability to resolve the lingering colonial question that is Western Sahara. It has destroyed the region's tourism industry, not to mention the livelihoods of families across the entire region, forcing hundreds of young men into the burgeoning smuggling and trafficking business for a living—who are then deemed "terrorist" by their nervous governments, which in turn receive arms from Washington to track them down.

Algeria, a major oil producer, a natural gas superpower, and once the headquarters of French colonialism in the region, (which also served as the chief overseas base for the Black Panther Party) has been critical in this entire process. It was there that Dick Cheney's Halliburton set up and registered as an indigenous company, then plunged into a maelstrom of fraud and corruption that ensnared important Algerians, helping to further destabilize a nation that sent many of its nationals in the 1980s to fight in Afghanistan—before returning in the 1990s to launch a war in their homeland.[26]

This is the background that sheds light on why U.S. imperialism has decided to establish AFRICOM, the African Command, which will target the continent. Slyly seeking to convert their disadvantage—participation in the African Slave Trade—into an asset, U.S. imperialism announced that General William E. 'Kip' Ward, the Army's only active black four-star general, would lead this newly formed intervention force. Ward earned his spurs commanding the occupation force after the breakup of Socialist Yugoslavia.[27]

Africa has not been impressed. Both Libya and Algeria reportedly told Washington that they would not host AFRICOM, as did Morocco, which had been thought to be a satrap of U.S. imperialism but, apparently is afraid to further alienate its populace, given the rank hostility toward Washington as a result of its wars in Iraq and Afghanistan.[28]

Perhaps even more critical is the staunch opposition by the continent's most populous nation and also a rich source of petroleum—Nigeria. One unnamed official was particularly resolute. His nation, it was announced, "is not going to allow the U.S. to establish any military base in the ECOWAS [Economic Community of West Africa] region. The interest of the U.S. government in the [oil-rich] Gulf of Guinea has reinforced the commitment of the government to intensify its efforts at providing the needed security in the sub-region."[29]

South Africa apparently is not happy either with AFRICOM, with their Defense Minister purportedly refusing to accept phone calls from General Ward. Mosiuoa Lekota told the press that "Africa has to avoid the presence of foreign forces on her soil" and insisted that this view would be backed up by the pan-continental African Union.[30] This is a reflection of the ramified military, intelligence and economic links that have served to bind Abuja and Pretoria, arguably the two most formidable African nations.[31]

Nonplussed by the prospect of confronting a united Africa allied with China and bolstered by Socialist Cuba, U.S. imperialism has not relinquished its demonic schemes. Suggestive in this regard is the direct intervention of U.S. imperialism on the continent, when Washington provided intelligence assistance and satellite imagery to Ethiopian forces when they toppled the so-called Islamic Courts Union in Mogadishu, Somalia in early 2007. As Africans fled in horror, U.S. AC-130 gun-ships took off from an airstrip in eastern Ethiopia and proceeded to rain down a hellfire of ammunition upon them. The back story is that Somalia was once ruled by Siad Barre, who was induced by U.S. imperialism in the 1970s to dump his Soviet allies in favor of a revanchist and irredentist war in the disputed Ogaden region against neighboring Ethiopia, then ruled by a leftist-regime. Predictably, his ultra-nationalism crumbled as the nation descended into the kind of shrinkage of government that the U.S. Republican Right has proclaimed is its ideal. As pointed out by Salim Lone, a former high-ranking UN official, U.S. imperialism in league with Ethiopia has established a version of the lawless Abu Ghraib and Guantanamo Bay in the region replete with kidnappings, extraordinary renditions (i.e. extreme kidnappings), secret prisons and countless numbers of "disappeared"—all justified in the name of the "global war on terror."[32]

As these outrages have occurred, U.S. imperialism has continued to hammer the government of Sudan because of real and imagined human rights violations in the Darfur region. In a harbinger of things to come, this problem has been laid at the doorstep of Beijing, a recipient of Sudanese petroleum, to the point where some are calling for a boycott of the 2008 Olympics—or the so-called "Genocide Olympics," as dubbed by the former paramour of Woody Allen, Mia Farrow—unless China somehow induces Khartoum to alter its policies. Her crusade has been joined by other celebrities, including the actors Don Cheadle and George Clooney, who have lobbied in foreign capitals. Even professional basketball players, like Tracy McGrady of the Houston Rockets and Ira Newble of the Cleveland Cavaliers—indeed, virtually the entire team excluding star hoopster, Le Bron James—have sought to "Save Darfur." [33]

To be sure, there are severe human rights violations in Darfur—and probably even worse transgressions can be ascribed directly to the government in neighboring Central African Republic, though for whatever reason this has not received the attention of some in the U.S., perhaps because it is not part of the Arab League. Still, the situation in Darfur cries out for resolution. Nevertheless, Michael Clough, a former official of the elite Council on Foreign Affairs in Manhattan, has argued that "genocide is not being committed in Darfur," [34] just as others have suggested that the number of deaths and displaced has likewise been exaggerated—for whatever reason. Agreeing with Clough is former Nigerian President Olusegun Obasanjo who declared, "What we know [about Darfur] is that there was an uprising, rebellion and the government armed another group of people to stop that rebellion. ....that does not amount to genocide from our own reckoning." The UN agreed. But as the Ugandan scholar, Mahmood Mamdani, pointed out, certain forces in the U.S. have been clamoring for military intervention by U.S. imperialism in Sudan—in order to halt "genocide"—by dint of redeploying U.S. forces from Iraq! [35]

Yet just as Swaziland—which does not happen to have a sizeable and obstreperous European minority—does not receive as much attention as Zimbabwe, though this smaller Southern African nation makes Harare shine in comparison, the incessant focus upon Sudan should be a cause for deeper reflection.

This reflection has happened—to an extent—though more often beyond these shores. Thus, in London's *Guardian* one writer was struck by the fact that in Sudan's neighbor, the Congo, 3 to 4 million have been killed in recent years compared with the estimated 200,000 civilian deaths in Darfur, yet the latter has been a cause celebre while the Congo crisis, by way of comparison, a tad obscure. Why? This analyst ascribes it is due in part to the fact that Darfur is easy to characterize as yet another example of the perfidy of "The Arabs." Perhaps the recent interest of Beijing in the Congo may inspire more concern for this troubled land by the acolytes of U.S. imperialism. [36]

Those familiar with the petroleum that drives U.S. imperialism should not be shocked to discover that this strategic fuel must be contemplated in divining Washington's policy toward Khartoum. On 3 March 2007 the *Los Angeles Times* reported that "the Sudanese government is quietly escalating oil exploration inside the Darfur region." This complements the oil discoveries in neighboring Chad—which are of sufficient dimension that this alone would have drawn Darfur from the shadows of obscurity. Sudan is also the largest nation by territory in Africa, a member of both the Arab League and the influential Organization of Islamic

Conference—and a former home of former U.S. ally, Osama Bin Laden. In fact, Khartoum has secretly worked with the CIA to spy on the insurgency in Iraq and has aided U.S. imperialism in Somalia—yet for whatever reasons, U.S. activists who target Darfur have not highlighted the malfeasance and nonfeasance of their own government in arresting this crisis.[37] Similarly, as a recent analysis suggests, the "Save Darfur" movement has "generally failed to emphasize this issue of fully funding the AU [African Union] [or] demanding more prominently a UN deployment...." [38] Likewise receiving insufficient scrutiny has been Washington's past backing of the recently settled insurgency in Southern Sudan (Darfur is in western Sudan), the presence of both Chevron and Exxon-Mobil just across the border in Chad, where they have invested billions and other "coincidental" occurrences.[39] Indeed, Africa now accounts for 30% of Exxon-Mobil's output.[40]

Sadly, the tragedy that is unfolding in Darfur has become yet another monument to the hypocrisy that has characterized Washington's policy toward Africa since the similarly tragic days of the African Slave Trade. This hypocrisy and double-dealing inheres in U.S. imperialism, which is grounded in the reality that for each dollar of net capital flowing into Sub-Saharan Africa from the rest of the world, $1.06 flows out: 51 cents through terms of trade losses (imbalanced trade rules that seek to keep a lid on the cost of commodities that Africa produces while imposing no price caps on the finished goods—trucks, tractors, etc.—that it buys); 25 cents through debt servicing and profit remittances; and 30 cents through leakages into capital outflows. This means a net transfer of resources from Africa to the rest of the world, especially to the home of U.S. imperialism and British neo-colonialism.[41]

Onerous loans are a basic reason why all too often more capital flows out of Africa than "in." This has spawned a mass global movement demanding that banks and the North Atlantic powers who profit from this system of inequity "drop the debt." Thus, Sub-Saharan Africa as a whole spends $13.3 billion repaying debts each year—while they need $15.5 billion each year to fight the spread of HIV-AIDS. Fortunately, these anti-debt activists have had measurable impact and, thus, point the way for others to follow. Thus, because of efforts to cancel debts, primary school enrollment in Uganda has doubled, 500,000 children in Mozambique have received vaccinations they would not have received otherwise, etc.[42]

But as to be expected, the doyens of death have not accepted this movement supinely. As Jesse Jackson put it, "they prey upon the poorest nations, taking resources from the most desperate peoples—billionaire scavengers pocketing the funds that might go to feed children whose families live on less than $1 a day. They are called the vulture funds. They protect their scavengings with fat checks to politicians and lobbyists. One of the leading vulture firms is led by major donors to President [sic] Bush." Thus, in 1979 the Romanian government lent Zambia money to buy Romanian tractors. Zambia was unable to earn the foreign exchange needed to pay for this and other debts. Thus, the two nations negotiated to liquidate the debt for $3 million. But then the vultures arrived, buying the debt from Romania for less than $4 million, then renegotiating with Zambian officials and—amid charges of bribery and abuse—cut a new deal on the debt. They are now suing the Zambian government for the original debt plus interest, which they calculate at over $40 million—and they expect to win. Unsurprisingly, the vultures—including the Bush crony, Paul Singer—are major donors to the GOP.[43]

Other than vulture funds and mining companies, U.S. based pharmaceutical companies—who have pioneered in the fleecing of U.S. patients and consumers—have been the most relentless in exploiting Africans. Emblematic is the fact that the biggest of "Big Pharma"—Pfizer—stands accused of killing and injuring dozens of Nigerian children by using them as research guinea pigs by rushing to market a controversially new and unapproved antibiotic.[44] This is not unusual. For example, when a charter member of Big Pharma produced a vaccine for rotavirus—a gastric infection that causes thousands of hospitalizations each year but very few deaths in the U.S.—that was linked an extremely rare but serious side effect in 1999, the company withdrew it from the market. But in the developing world, where rotavirus causes as many as 500,000 deaths a year, GlaxoSmithKline sought regulatory approval for its vaccine in Mexico.[45]

Needless to say, their policies have been worse in relatively underdeveloped Africa. For years, Big Pharma simply refused treatment to those victimized by HIV-AIDS in Africa; those with this disease were simply unable to afford the $12,000 a year required for the drug cocktails that enable many to survive. When African nations made noises about finding ways to provide the drugs more cheaply, Washington—the mouthpiece for Big Pharma, the drug arm of U.S. imperialism—threatened trade sanctions and forced them to back down.[46] Accompanying this deadly assault, the Bush administration's chief foreign aid official, argued that it would be too costly to treat and care for the tens of millions of Africans living with HIV-AIDS by dint of antiretroviral drugs since—allegedly—these patients "don't know what Western time is" and, therefore, are unable to utilize a regime that calls for ingesting of medicine every few hours.[47] Thankfully, this misguided man came under a hailstorm of criticism and was compelled to backtrack.

Though invoking of patent and intellectual property laws protecting

"Big Pharma" has been done repeatedly to the detriment of Africans, this has not kept the North Atlantic powers from ignoring such legalities when deemed necessary. Thus, in the aftermath of the Fall 2001 anthrax scare in the U.S., Washington threatened to override Bayer Corporation's patent on Cipro, which has proved effective in fighting this disease. This was done, although African nations who have sought to override intellectual property restrictions to confront the HIV-AIDS emergency have been threatened with legal action.[48]

The World Trade Organization is among the chief enforcers of such law-driven hypocrisy but as bad as they are, they may be exceeded in deadliness by the International Monetary Fund and World Bank, the enforcers of the discredited "Washington Consensus" of deregulation and privatization, nostrums that have suffocated many an African nation. For example, after being battered by a 16-year-long brutal conflict, fueled in no minor way by the U.S. right-wing, who were upset by the nation's socialist-oriented path of development, Mozambique felt compelled to adopt "free market" policies. Thus, Maputo was compelled by the IMF and WB to drop policies designed to assist workers in one of their main industries—cashews. Predictably, this destroyed the industry, and wrecked the lives of countless workers and peasants.[49]

But like a mad scientist, the IMF has continued to engage in experiments in Africa that are strangling the patient. Thus, only recently, this agency has been criticized for requiring policies which require poorer nations e.g. Malawi, to freeze or curtail recruitment of teachers in an attempt to curtail spending.[50] Even the former chief economist of the World Bank, Nobel Laureate Joseph Stiglitz, has condemned his former employer, accusing it of lack of transparency (while it preaches the opposite message to Africa), not to mention bad economic policy.[51] Reform of both is made difficult because by encrusted custom the IMF is headed by a Western European and the WB is headed by a U.S. national. Ironically, this means that an African, not to mention a Canadian or Australian or Russian or Chinese or Japanese—irrespective of talent and qualification—are unable to head these two important agencies. It is little wonder that thousands have marched against their existence. Thus, when Horst Koehler, the German only recently appointed, showed his face in Johannesburg during the Summer of 2000, he received a hostile response, led by the South African Communist Party. They well recalled that when the previous apartheid regime began to sell state assets to white-owned conglomerates and raised interest rates to the highest level in the nation's history, the IMF was prodding it to do so. During the dying days of the apartheid regime, the IMF granted Pretoria a sizeable $750 million loan, which carried conditions such as a lowered budget deficit to prevent a new democratic government from spending more on social programs and wages for civil servants. For a South African militant analyzing this dire situation, the causes were clear. "One reason for the IMF's crisis of legitimacy," argued Trevor Ngwane, "is the control exercised by the U.S. government.." He hailed the "30,000 people [who] joined in a protest" against the IMF and WB in April 2000—and pledged to duplicate their militancy.[52]

Just as deadly an assault on Africa has been launched by agribusiness. Periodically—not least due to the devastation engendered by imperialism and neo-colonialism—famines erupt on the continent. On these sad occasions, Archer Daniels Midland, a major funder of Presidents and Congresspersons alike, usually emerges wealthier. This is why CARE, the huge poverty-relief organization, stopped taking $45 million annually in indirect food aid from the U.S. government, since that immense amount is used to buy food from the likes of ADM, which is then given to CARE dispatched by U.S. shipping interests. Then the food is not delivered to the poverty-stricken but, instead, is sold on the open local market for the highest price possible—the "free market" in operation. The resultant revenue—which is about 75% of the original aid money—is used to fund programs for the poor and hungry. This scenario is a microcosm of the various subsidies provided to U.S. agri-business involved in corn, soy, cotton, rice and sugar production that are insistently and uncompromisingly driving African farmers out of business.[53] Big Pharma and Agribusiness are essential components of the iron cage constructed by U.S. imperialism that is killing the dreams—and the bodies—of countless Africans.

This is why Washington was terribly displeased when South Africa—the natural leader of the continent, given its development and the sophistication of its trade unions and political parties—began to challenge Big Pharma, then agricultural subsidies. This was after the Bush regime's May 2002 announcement that it would seek a 67% increase in U.S. subsidies to agribusiness over the next decade. This is not minor for Africa since agriculture accounts for 70% of the continent's employment, 40% of its exports and 35% of its GDP. Joining South Africa's crusade were Thailand, China, Brazil, Argentina, and CARICOM (the 15-nation Caribbean community). Stung, even the IMF and World Bank criticized these subsidies.[54]

What all this reveals is that the much ballyhooed foreign aid, which demagogic politicians often point to as absorbing tax dollars, is more mirage than substance. To begin with, it is a minor part of the U.S. budget and, in any case, a good deal of what is called "foreign aid" consists of spending on U.S.-based consultants, training and research. In other words, U.S. "foreign aid" in Africa is too often spent on high salaries being paid to expatriate consultants—who carry U.S. passports.[55] The U.S. Agency for International Development concedes openly on its website that "the principal beneficiary of America's foreign assistance program has always been the United States." Thus, 53 cents of every dollar spent by the U.S. in tackling the HIV-AIDS crisis in Africa never left the Washington, D.C., metropolitan area.[56]

The good news for Africa is that the other Asian giant—India—which has many descendants residing in Indian Ocean port cities ranging from Durban to Mombasa, is also taking more of an interest in Africa. Indian movies have been popular in Africa for some time. India's state-owned Oil and Natural Gas Corporation produces petroleum in Sudan, and Indian investment in the former Ivory Coast is expected to grow to $1 billion by 2011. Indian diplomatic missions will open soon in Mali, Gabon, Niger and Burkina Faso. Inexorably this interest by China, then India, will help in curbing the worst excesses of U.S. imperialism.[57]

Also heartening is a trend of historically profound proportion. W.E.B. Du Bois is widely known as the "Father of Pan-Africanism," and practiced what he preached when he migrated to newly independent Ghana, where he passed away in August, 1963, as the March on Washington—to be addressed famously by Martin Luther King, Jr.—heralded a new era. Du Bois was the living embodiment of a trend that is flowering today and does not bode well for U.S. imperialism. The mutual attraction that is developing between Africans in the diaspora—particularly African-Americans—and progressive Africa is the worst news for the U.S. right-wing since the demise of the African Slave Trade. The African Union, the pan-continental body based in Ethiopia, which foresees eventual economic and political integration of the 53 independent African nations, not unlike its equivalent, the European Union, has been essential in promoting this welcome trend. The AU has reached out explicitly to the Diaspora, including CARICOM, which—unbeknownst to many—is one of the more progressive formations on the planet, befitting a body that includes the descendants of Cheddi Jagan of Guyana and Michael Manley of Jamaica.[58]

The descendants of the enslaved Africans who enriched U.S. imperialism have moved aggressively into the global arena in order to vindicate their just claims for reparations. Aetna has been accused of insuring the lives of slaves for their owners. JP Morgan Chase and Bank of America also have been accused of profiting from human bondage,[59] as has Barclays Bank.[60] Support from the international community—particularly the AU and CARICOM—will be indispensable to the vindication of claims for reparations.

This coming together of progressive Africans trans-nationally will also be a vindication of the vision of Du Bois, and a further marker in the slow but steady decline of U.S. imperialism.

7: U.S. Imperialism Unbound?

Both Washington and Wall Street were worried.

It was the dog days of a brutal summer, August 2007, but the sun's persistent rays were not the sole reason for the rivulets of perspiration rolling down the frowning faces of the self-proclaimed "masters of the universe." For the "cowboy capitalism" that reigns in the U.S. inexorably had engendered yet another "panic" leading to mass unemployment, evictions and crumpled lives. But that was not all.

For years the ruling class had dismissed concerns about the trillions of dollars that the U.S. owes China, Japan, South Korea and the Gulf nations led by Saudi Arabia, arguing that these debts gave no undue leverage to foreign governments. Yet in the midst of a global financial meltdown that had "Made in USA" written all over it, palpable fear had arisen that the lengthening line of foreign creditors of this nation were converting their dollars into investment funds to acquire companies, real estate, banks and other assets of the U.S.—and elsewhere. It is feared that these "Sovereign Wealth Funds," which control trillions of dollars in investments, are contradicting the gospel of privatization—demanding that other nations sell their government-owned industries—by engaging in cross-border investments that amount to cross-border nationalizations of U.S. assets by foreign governments.[1]

What concerned the myrmidons of finance capital is that as this worrying prospect was escalating, masses abroad were rallying against the titans of Wall Street, their hedge funds portrayed as "locusts." Their lack of transparency, asset-stripping ("strip and flip," the apparent fate of Chrysler), loading up debt upon the backs of fragile businesses—all are viewed with increasing disdain, notably in Western Europe.[2] With good reason, Wall Street and Washington were beginning to feel besieged, a feeling not assuaged by the steadily descending stock market.

The diminishing prestige of U.S. imperialism, sinking like its military in the quagmire of Iraq, was beginning to embolden those who heretofore had been viewed as lapdogs. The International Monetary Fund, a fierce Doberman when it came to monitoring the financial health of developing nations but typically a toothless terrier when it came to confronting U.S. imperialism, was beginning to change its tune. In the Spring of 2006, the IMF clearly irritated the Bush regime when it faulted Washington for its budget and trade deficits, its failure to provide universal health care and its prediction that the much-vaunted dollar would inevitably decline in value against the world's other currencies.[3]

This rebuke was further evidence—as if any were needed—that the world was tiring of playing the role of U.S. imperialism's charge card. Thus in 2003, because of the current account deficit, the U.S. needed to entice $531 billion from the rest of the world—and actually got $747 billion. For 2004, the need was $666 billion—it actually got $915 billion. For 2005, the need was $801 billion; $1.025 trillion was actually received. But, as the saying goes, this is not sustainable, which means it cannot continue—the rest of the world either will not or cannot keep sending billions to a profligate U.S. imperialism which refuses to put its house in order. Thus, from a high of receiving $117.2 billion in August 2005, there has been a steady decline in foreign inflows, down to $74 billion in December 2005 and $78 billion for January 2006. For the longest, Uncle Sam has traveled around the world like a deranged panhandler, rattling a tin cup in one hand with an Uzi sub machine gun in the other, demanding tribute. Increasingly, this crude robbery is becoming unsustainable.

If U.S. imperialism is to continue receiving gobs of capital, particularly for Treasury bills necessary for everything from the funding of the military to health sciences research, interest rates will have to rise—but in order to give a jolt to a foot-dragging economy, the Federal Reserve Bank has been moving in the opposite direction. All this may lead to a sharp selloff in the dollar—as has been happening for some time in the dollar-euro market, at least since November 2005. As this occurs, these foreign currencies—particularly the euro but also the yen and other competitive currencies—will appreciate in value and the dollar will fall, leading to price increases in the value of imports, e.g. Toyotas and cameras, gasoline at the pump, and computers, and creating the worse nightmare for a central banker of U.S. imperialism: inflation amidst a stagnating economy and a likely recession, if not the "D-word" (depression). If this were to occur as the rest of the world "decouples" from a sagging U.S. imperialism, this could spur a "new world order"—though not necessarily what George H.W. Bush had in mind when he enunciated this concept.[4]

Already inter-imperialist rivalry—which unleashed the "war to end all wars" in 1914—is becoming hard to contain. In January 2001, well before the wars in Iraq and Afghanistan signaled the relative decline of U.S. imperialism, Japan and France joined hands urging Asian economies to include the euro and the yen in a new managed currency regime, arguing that excessive reliance on the dollar had brought disaster.[5] Asian nations hardly needed prompting from Paris and Tokyo to read what was obvious even to those lacking powers of acute discernment: In the Summer of 2006 the United Arab Emirates—groaning under the weight of cash reserves—confirmed that a strategic decision had been made to move $10 billion of its $29 billion in foreign exchange reserves into euros.[6] This could not have come at a worse moment for U.S. imperialism. As of February 2007, fresh figures indicated the first net capital outflow from the U.S. in two years, as foreign purchases of long-term securities plunged 95% to $2.5 billion in December of the preceding year. This unexpected loss of capital underlined the uncertainty over foreign willingness to continue financing the U.S. current account deficit, which has been supported by strong demand for U.S. Treasury notes from Asian central banks in particular.[7]

It is difficult to over-estimate the significance of what is happening to the dollar. Dollar hegemony has been essential to U.S. imperialism. With the 1971 abandonment of the Bretton Woods regime and suspension of the dollar's peg to the value of gold, the denomination of oil prices in dollars, then the eased cross-border flow of currencies facilitated by computerization, all central banks have felt obliged to hold more dollars than they otherwise need, particularly to ward off sudden speculative attacks on their currencies in financial markets. Dollar reserves—virtually by definition—can only be invested in U.S. assets; thus dollar hegemony prevents the exporting nations from spending domestically the dollars they earn from the U.S. trade deficit and forces them to finance the U.S. capital account, thus shipping real wealth to the U.S. in exchange for the privilege of financing U.S. debt to further the U.S. economy. The U.S. capital account in turn finances the U.S. trade deficit. Further, any asset, regardless of location, that is denominated in dollars is a U.S. asset in essence. When oil is denominated in dollars through U.S. state action and the dollar is a fiat currency, the U.S. in essence owns the world's oil for free. This is a scam that would do Ponzi or the Mafia proud. Washington seeks to "improve" on it by driving down further the exchange rate of the dollar to erode the value of the massive dollar holdings of its trade partners— notably China and Japan.

Tokyo's foreign exchange reserves alone were valued at $830 billion by September 2004—much more than what the Marshall Plan lent Europe (in adjusted terms). Yet Japan did not get any real benefits because their de facto loans to U.S. imperialism were denominated in dollars, which Washington can print at will. Dollars are veritably useless in Japan unless converted to yen, which because of dollar hegemony, Japan is not in a position to do without reducing the yen money supply, causing the Japanese economy to contract and the yen exchange rate to rise, thus harming Japanese export competitiveness. Thus, as the economist Henry Chu, put it, "dollar hegemony has gone beyond the 'too big to fail' syndrome. It has created a world of willing slaves to defend the dollar out of fear that without a strong dollar, tomorrow's food may not be available."

As Chu sees it, U.S. imperialism's tie-up with Beijing—a direct outgrowth of Cold War anti-Sovietism—suggests that if the Chinese economy hits a brick wall, as it very well may when the U.S. debt bubble bursts (which is happening) and Chinese exports to the U.S. fall drastically, Chinese sovereign debt will lose credit rating, causing yuan interest rates to rise, causing more hot money to flow into China, causing the central bank there to buy more U.S. Treasury bills, forcing dollar interest rates to fall. More hot money flows to Beijing are creating a financial hurricane that will make the 1997 Asian financial crisis seem like an impotent April shower.[8]

Part of the construction of U.S. hegemony in the hemisphere is encouraging nations in the Americas to adopt the dollar as their currency. When El Salvador did this in 2001, it not only suggested that it had become the "51st state," but also marked the beginning of a deepening crisis for a small Central American nation that had already suffered tremendously after a direct U.S. military intervention during the Reagan era. For this currency switch drove up the prices of many staples, as producers and merchants rounded up to the nearest nickel, dime or quarter—but worker salaries did not keep pace. Following Panama, which has been a member of the dollar club for a century—since it became an independent nation, seceding from neighboring Colombia, due to the shenanigans of U.S. imperialism—El Salvador quickly discovered the bitter news of life under the hegemony of Washington and Wall Street: the poorer you are, the worse it is.[9]

As if the exploitation of poor El Salvador is insufficient, a movement is afoot to impose a free trade agreement, sweeping from the Yukon to the Yucatan to Patagonia. But as Harlem Congressman Charles Rangel bluntly put it, "there are some people who hate unions so much, they can't see their way clear to supporting [any] provision" that bolsters labor rights. Rangel simply insists that these agreements include labor protections adopted by the International Labor Organization, but the Bush regime, backed by Big Business, has insisted that this could lead to the overturning of U.S. labor practices, or that Hugo Chavez or Evo Morales might seek to overturn anti-union laws in North Carolina. As ever, U.S. imperialism which sits unsteadily on the right of the global political spectrum, is stoutly resisting being dragged into the international mainstream.[10]

Along with "dollarization" and rigged "free trade" schemes, privatization has been the other elixir prescribed by the snake-oil salesmen that predominate in the U.S. This has not only afflicted small nations in the hemisphere but has also been adopted by the once mighty British, notably under the rule of Reagan's soul-mate, Margaret Thatcher. Thus, British Rail has been sacrificed to the gods of privatization—a switch from a publicly owned railway. The result has been chaos, an awesome decline in the quality of passenger service, frequent delays and cancellations, rising fares—and worse; i.e. it has mirrored the experiment with the other half of the quack-medicine regime—deregulation—as experienced by U.S. airlines. In 1997 California was induced to deregulate its power industry. The now infamous Enron pounced, and soon Golden Staters were hit with a double whammy of rising prices and reduced services—including repetitive blackouts and brownouts.[11]

But instead of engaging in an agonizing reappraisal of the poisonous medicines that have led to the relative decline of U.S. imperialism—privatization, deregulation, military misadventures, the rise in influence of conservative hawks, and the like—instead the finger of accusation increasingly is being pointed abroad, notably in the direction of Beijing. The present head of the ostensible policeman of Wall Street, the Securities and Exchange Commission's Christopher Cox, made headlines as a Congressman when in 1999 he reported on alleged Chinese military links to basic U.S. commercial and financial activities. Supposedly, U.S. capital markets were being used to finance Chinese weapons development and proliferation. This was no way to treat a major creditor but, oblivious, the influential Congressman Frank Wolf followed up by issuing stern warnings that led to the Russian oil company, Lukoil, announcing that it was transferring its listing on the New York Stock Exchange to London, as did the Canadian oil company, Talisman, which was being pressured to pull out of the Sudan.[12]

This was occurring as London—not least due to U.S. imperialism over-estimating its mettle—was surpassing New York as a global financial center, the implications of which have yet to be totaled. In January 2007 the International Capital Markets Association announced that some 49% of new international bond issues in the preceding year were euro-denominated; nearly twice the proportion conducted in dollars.[13]

In short, if U.S. imperialism were seeking scapegoats, it could just as easily look across the Atlantic as the Pacific. But China, ruled by those not of European descent and by Communists to boot, makes a much juicier target. Thus, in the Spring of 2005, the Bush regime warned Beijing that it could be cited as a currency manipulator and face economic sanctions unless it moved swiftly to overhaul its currency system. Democrats and Republicans alike have charged that China's valuation of its currency puts

U.S. companies at a huge competitive disadvantage and has contributed to the loss of U.S. factory jobs. As Washington sees it, the yuan is undervalued by 40%, which makes Chinese goods cheaper in the U.S., and U.S. products more expensive in China. Before this dangerous warning to Beijing, the Senate by a lopsided 67-33 vote moved toward passing legislation that would impose across-the-board 27.5% tariffs on all Chinese imports to the U.S.—unless its currency regime is altered.[14]

The problem in confronting Beijing on this and other issues is the disunity within the U.S. ruling class itself on this bedrock measure. This contrasts sharply with the Cold War against Moscow, where unity reigned. Thus, smaller U.S. manufacturers are irked by the trade imbalance with China and are demanding action, while some of their larger counterparts are benefiting from the undervalued yuan. "China is waging a mercantile war," fumed M. Brian O'Shaughnessy, president of Revere Copper Products in Rome, New York, "and we're being pacifists." China has split the usually unified National Association of Manufacturers.[15]

Beijing no doubt wonders what else it needs to do to placate U.S. imperialism. Already it is lending billions to the U.S., while absorbing the political pain of containing an often restive working class. One analyst has spoken of Washington as the "New Rome," with China being chief among the "vassal states kept perpetually at the level of subsistence poverty" due to "payments of tribute." Imports from China are resold in the U.S. at a greater profit margin for U.S. importers than that enjoyed by Beijing exporters in producing for export; a $2 toy leaving a Chinese factory is a $3 part of a shipment arriving in Long Beach. By the time it is bought by the U.S. consumer, it costs $10, as the U.S. economy registers $10 in final sales, less $3 in imports, for a $7 addition to GDP.[16]

Yet the tribute paid by Beijing to the U.S. ruling elite is increasingly deemed to be insufficient, thus the vote to slap a punitive tariff on Chinese exports. That this could unleash a foreseeable chain of events that ultimately would punish U.S. imperialism severely has been lost in a tidal wave of China-bashing.

This attempt by U.S. imperialism to bully the most populous nation in the world, an Asian juggernaut bristling with nuclear weapons, is an indication of both its arrogance and desperation as it endures its relative decline. After seizing office, the Bush leaguers mounted a blitzkrieg against international law, repudiating the Kyoto Protocol on Global Warming, the International Criminal Court, the Comprehensive Test Ban Treaty, an international convention to regulate the trade in small arms, a verification protocol for the Biological Weapons Convention, an international convention to regulate and reduce smoking, the World Conference Against Racism in Durban and the Anti-Ballistic Missile Systems Treaty, among others. Perhaps more chilling was the early 2002 decision by the White House to draw up war plans for a nuclear first-strike against seven states—the so-called "axis of evil" (Iran, Iraq and North Korea); Libya and Syria—and Russia and China.[17] It seemed that even then, U.S. imperialism was unbound, not tethered to the rule of law.

Conventional wisdom holds that the tragic events of 11 September 2001 motivated this demented approach to international law and security, but the fact is that most of these measures were instituted before this pivotal date. In any case, international law has a regimen that would have allowed for dealing with the tragic consequences of that fateful day; but just as the U.S. Supreme Court refused to follow the outline of the U.S. Constitution in the Bush v. Gore decision of December 2000, which handed the White House to the Bush leaguers, the Bush regime refused to adhere to the protocol laid out by law in the aftermath of the attack on Manhattan. Thus, the 1971 Montreal Sabotage Convention provided a comprehensive framework for dealing with Washington's 2001 confrontation with Kabul, just as the UN Charter and the Kellogg-Briand Pact of 1928 mandated a peaceful resolution of this bilateral dispute. The dispute could have been submitted to the International Court of Justice at The Hague. Instead, the war option was chosen and U.S. imperialism remains bogged down in Afghanistan, and has dragged in other North Atlantic powers as well, so that Iraq could then be invaded.

Still, it remains true that the Bush regime escalated its lawless bravado in the aftermath of 9/11. It was not just the tapping of phones and the passage of the so-called Patriot Act, it was also the lawlessness with which the rest of the world was handled. The U.S. Supreme Court, not known nowadays as a bastion of progressivism, did rule in 2006 in *Hamdan v. Rumsfeld* that Common Article 3 of the Geneva Convention applies to the conflict with Al Qaeda—a holding that makes high-ranking Bush regime officials potentially subject to war crimes prosecution under the federal War Crimes Act.[18]

Apparently unbothered by the spectacle of being measured for orange jumpsuits, the Bush leaguers proceeded to issue National Security Presidential Directive/NSPD 51 and the Homeland Security Presidential Directive/HSPD-20, which provide the basis for an augmentation of power in the White House that is veritably dictatorial. That is, if a "decapitating event" occurred in the U.S. that somehow incapacitates the federal government, all power and decision making would devolve to the White House.[19]

This breathtaking grab for power is of a piece with the chilling events that U.S. imperialism has orchestrated in Europe. The Council of Europe in June 2007 provided a bleak description of secret prisons run by the CIA in Eastern Europe. Prisoners guarded by silent men in black masks and dark visors were held naked in cramped cells and shackled to walls, according to the lead investigator for this 46-nation rights group. Ventilation holes in the cells release bursts of hot or freezing air—temperature used as a form of extreme pressure to wear down prisoners. Prisoners were subjected to "water-boarding," a form of simulated drowning—i.e. torture—and relentless blasts of music and sound from rap to loud laughter to screams. These prisons were operated in Poland and Romania from 2003 to 2006. Now that these Eastern European nations have escaped the grasp of the "Iron Curtain" and "Soviet domination," they are free to take their presumed rightful place as flunkies of U.S. imperialism.[20]

To be fair, U.S. imperialism is treating a good deal of Europe beyond the Danube as its personal preserve. Thus, the CIA has carried out more than 1,000 undeclared flights over European territory between 2001 and 2006, mostly involving the rendition of "terror suspects." This is all in putative violation of international air treaties requiring airlines to declare routes and stopovers for planes on such missions.[21] Besides, the tiny island of Diego Garcia, in the Indian Ocean, was used for processing these "detainees."[22] Little wonder that the UN Human Rights Committee demanded the immediate closure of secret U.S. detention facilities.[23]

An outraged Europe has struck back, with Germany recommending that prosecutors issue arrest warrants for 13 U.S. intelligence operatives in connection with kidnappings of suspects, including the beating and detention of a German citizen. According to Khaled Masri, a German national of Lebanese descent, he was pulled off a bus on New Year's Eve 2003 as he was crossing the Serbian border into Macedonia. On holiday, he was seized by Macedonian officials and driven to the capital, Skopje, where he was interrogated for days and accused of being an extremist. He was threatened at gunpoint and denied access to German consular officials. Seven to eight men dressed in black and wearing masks beat him relentlessly. He went on a hunger strike for 37 days before he was released in the mountains of Albania.[24] At home, the American Civil Liberties Union has sued a Boeing subsidiary for allegedly helping the CIA with this "extraordinary rendition" program.[25] "This is the first time we are accusing a blue-chip American company of profiting from torture," ACLU lawyer Ben Wizner said.[26]

Masri's experience mirrors that of Maher Arar, a software engineer of Syrian origin who holds Canadian nationality, who was wrongly deported from the U.S. to Syria (while in transit to Canada), where he was imprisoned and tortured for a year.[27] Lately, U.S. imperialism's lawless swagger has exceeded its normal bounds: a former executive at a British manufacturing company has become the first British national to be the subject of an extradition request from the U.S. that did not require the U.S. to prove there was a case to answer. He is also the first example of the U.S. seeking to extradite a British citizen on anti-trust charges. While a British attempt to extradite a U.S. national to London requires "probable cause," there is no reciprocity in that there is a lower standard in reverse. If allies are being treated so shabbily—indeed, the partner in an alleged "special relationship"—one can only imagine how those who do not claim this exalted status are treated.[28] This lawlessness is a major reason why U.S. imperialism is so wildly unpopular nowadays, particularly in the North Atlantic where its allies are said to be sited. Yet it was former British Foreign Secretary, Robin Cook, who in the Spring of 2005, assailed the Bush regime for its cavalier approach to law and treaties, pointing to its attempt to scuttle the nuclear non-proliferation pact—while simultaneously seeking to bar Iran from developing civilian nuclear energy.[29]

In fact the abject lawlessness of U.S. imperialism's mass kidnappings and mass torture—prettily called "extraordinary rendition"—has complicated Washington's ability to rally the international community against Iran. Even the American Bar Association, usually somnolent when it comes to the protection of rights, voted in August 2007 to urge Congress to override a Bush regime order authorizing the CIA to use interrogation techniques such as water-boarding and sensory and sleep deprivation.[30] This was preceded—and perhaps prompted—by the call of six leading human rights groups (including Amnesty International and the Center for Constitutional Rights) for an end to the secret detention of suspects.[31]

What U.S. imperialism has wrought can be seen in the sad case of Jose Padilla, a U.S. national arrested in May 2002 at Chicago's O'Hare airport amid blaring charges about his supposedly being on the verge of detonating a "dirty bomb." He was taken to a navy brig in South Carolina, where he was kept in a tiny cell with no natural light, no clock and no calendar. He was kept there for over 1300 days. He was bombarded with harsh lights and pounding sounds. This torture prevented his meaningful participation in his own defense—and he was convicted, though not of the charge on which he was detained originally. According to James Yee, a former Army [Muslim] chaplain at Guantanamo, there is an entire section of the prison called Delta Block for detainees who have been reduced to a delusional state.[32]

Along with Abu Ghraib, the prison horror exposed by CBS-News' Dan Rather, (who was sacked shortly thereafter, after narrating a story about Bush's evasion of his National Guard duties) Guantanamo—or "Gitmo"—has become the symbol for U.S. imperialism's flagrant disregard of universally accepted norms. It represented a "travesty of justice," according to the *Financial Times*.[33] It was a "national disgrace," said the *New York Times*.[34] That it was. However, it was also a reflection of U.S. imperialism's siege mentality and incapability of finding a way out of the crisis in which it finds itself enmeshed. Worse is the fact that leading Republicans—presidential candidates and congressional leaders alike— refuse to renounce the torturous tactics deployed at Gitmo and, indeed, call for an expansion of such![35]

The increasingly isolated conservative hawks, and the Bush regime that represents them, are besieged on domestic and global fronts. Their ideology and praxis are attracting fewer and fewer and, therefore, they feel obliged to act ever more desperately and adventurously to attain their crazed goals. Like a latter day King Canute, they have stood on the shores of this land and sought to repel waves of sanity and progressivism. Thus, the White House has sought to limit the ability of foreign nationals to obtain judgments against despots and trans-national corporations in U.S. courts, arguing that such lawsuits have become a threat to U.S. foreign policy and could undermine the so-called war against terrorism. For the past two decades, federal courts have allowed victims of torture and other abuse to file claims under an otherwise obscure 1789 statute for violations of human rights norms, commonly known as the Alien Tort Claims Act. There is a fear in official Washington that this law will be used in claims against the U.S. itself; for example, the statute has been employed by a group of detainees in Guantanamo Bay, Cuba, who were captured in Afghanistan, and by a Mexican doctor who was kidnapped by bounty hunters and brought to the U.S. to stand trial in the killing of a drug agent. What concerns Big Business and their White House ally came clear in September 2002 when a federal appeals court ruled that trans-national corporations can be held liable in U.S. courts for aiding and abetting human rights violations committed by others abroad. This opinion emerged in a case involving Unocal Corporation, accused of turning a blind eye to human rights abuses, including murder and rape, against villagers in Myanmar. In the majority opinion, two judges said Unocal should be held to an international law standard developed by recent war crimes tribunals in Yugoslavia and Rwanda. The ruling may encourage Big Business to apply U.S. workplace standards to operations abroad.[36]

Consequently, when the case was appealed, the government filed a brief in the U.S. Court of Appeals for the Ninth Circuit in San Francisco; this case involved a Unocal Corporation gas pipeline in Myanmar [Burma]. In 2002 the State Department's top legal officer asked a federal judge to dismiss a lawsuit under the Alien Tort Act against Exxon-Mobil in connection with operations in Indonesia. Before that, Bush's ideological forefather—Ronald Reagan—filed a brief opposing use of the statute in a lawsuit against Ferdinand Marcos of the Philippines.[37]

Suggestive of the extreme nature of the Bush regime's views is that even the U.S. Supreme Court, not exactly regarded as a citadel of forward-thinking, has begun to break ranks on pressing global matters. In November 2005, then Attorney General Alberto R. Gonzalez chided Justices Stephen G. Breyer and Anthony M. Kennedy by name for using the opinions of foreign courts for guidance in rulings on constitutional cases. The fact is that the rest of the world is to the left of the U.S. and, therefore, judges looking abroad for guidance is generally a trend to be welcomed. Strikingly, on the current court, it is the conservative bloc — Samuel Alito, John Roberts, Antonin Scalia and Clarence Thomas — who oppose the use of foreign law in constitutional interpretation. These citations are notably timely in confronting matters e.g. "extraordinary rendition" and the treatment of prisoners at Guantanamo, along with the death penalty and the human rights of gays and lesbians.[38]

Surely, progressive activists must be careful not to engage in a kind of "legal imperialism" in handling sensitive matters. That explosive accusation was made after a Native American grouping in the U.S. sued successfully a Canadian smelter in U.S. courts because of damage said to have been inflicted on this side of the border. Yet remaining alert to the possibility of overreaching helps to insure that not only legal — but political — niceties are observed.[39] This must be kept foremost in mind when considering U.S. relations with its neighbors, since Canadians have yet to forget that Washington sought to conquer this vast land during the War of 1812, and Mexico is unable to forget how the 1846 war led to the loss of California and a good deal of its territory.

It is possible that the Bush regime's indifference to international law and global norms has its most dangerous impact when it comes to the environment. Once it was said that the question of peace is the paramount issue since a nuclear war could destroy humanity. Today we know that the same can be said about environmental challenges — particularly climate change — which, conceivably, could be as deadly as nuclear weapons. Still, there is no distinction in terms of the source of the main danger to humanity at this juncture: U.S. imperialism.

For it is not only the main source of nuclear proliferation and remains the only nation to have used this doomsday weapon, it now stands exposed as the chief threat to the fragile environment of our small planet. This issue, along with the lawless approach to human rights and the closely allied issue of wars in Iraq and Afghanistan, as much as anything else helps to explain why U.S. imperialism finds itself so isolated globally. This emerged dramatically and ironically at the White House itself when in a vain attempt to derail ongoing talks at the UN on climate change, the

Bush leaguers convened their own gathering in Washington. This end run around the UN was snuffed out in that Bush, according to the *Guardian* of London, was "castigated by European diplomats and found himself isolated...after a special conference on climate change ended without any progress. European ministers, diplomats and officials attending the Washington conference were scathing, particularly in private, over Mr. Bush's failure once again to commit to binding action on climate change." Even London is demanding mandatory targets for reducing greenhouse emissions, but Bush refuses.[40]

This was nothing new. Weeks after seizing power, Bush's decision to reject the Kyoto Protocol, "provoked a stunned and angry reaction...among America's allies in Europe and Japan;" yet, the White House officials reaffirmed that for them, Kyoto was dead.[41] Again, in May 2007, the Bush regime "in unusually harsh language," rejected a German proposal to confront climate change, which "has left many European diplomats furious." [42] Unfortunately, Bush is reflecting a portion of public opinion within the class he represents. In May 2007 only 3 out of 62 North American airline executives surveyed thought environmental concerns were a challenge, compared to 31 out of 72 airline executives in Europe, the Middle East and Africa, who described environmental issues as one of their most profound challenges. The stunned British Minister of the Environment, Ian Pearson, was irate, terming U.S. airlines as "completely irresponsible"—as he threatened legal action.[43]

Like a latter day Nero, Bush is fiddling while the planet burns. In February 2007, a panel of leading climate scientists warned of a future characterized by extreme weather events—long and intense droughts, fierce hurricanes, heat-waves and rising sea levels—as a result of rising temperatures driven by greenhouse emissions. This presents a clear and present danger not only to Caribbean islands and Africa, but also to Hawaii and coastal cities like San Francisco and San Diego.[44] Climate change, according to the UN Intergovernmental Panel on Climate Change, could lead to 50 million new refugees by 2010. Unless aggressive action is taken quickly, we face a frightening picture of a world of starvation, mass migration, rampant disease and the extinction of numerous animal species. Diseases such as malaria, dengue fever, yellow fever and Nile fever would spread. Wildfires would spin out of control and plant pests associated with warmer temperatures would spread.[45] It is possible that within decades hundreds of millions of people will not have enough water. Africa and Latin America would be affected most severely, thus locking in—actually worsening—the ordinary exploitation of U.S. imperialism.[46] A quarter of Africa's population lives within 100 kilometers of the sea coast.[47] Credible hope remains that human intervention can arrest these coming disasters—but Bush won't budge and the international community's anger rises accordingly.[48]

Instead, the White House is pushing the idea of bio-fuels—i.e. ethanol and the like—as a way to reduce greenhouse emissions. But this, too, has engendered a furious response. "Transforming food into fuels is a monstrosity," argues President Fidel Castro of Cuba. "Capitalism is preparing to perpetrate a massive euthanasia on the poor, and particularly on the poor of the South, " he said, "since it is there that the greatest reserves of the earth's biomass required to produce bio-fuels are found." [49] From the other shore, a recent analysis in the bourgeois journal, *Foreign Affairs*, suggested that "filling the 25-gallon tank of an SUV with pure ethanol requires over 450 pounds of corn—which contains enough calories to feed one person for a year." As more acres are planted with corn—the bio-fuel of choice in the U.S., unlike sugar which has propelled Brazil into global leadership in this fraught field—land will have to be pulled from other crops or environmentally fragile areas. Nevertheless, hedge funds are making huge bets on corn and in Bush-land, what they want, they get. Corn, in any case, has been stressed as the prime bio-fuel, due to adroit lobbying by Archer Daniels Midland, the biggest ethanol producer in the U.S. market.[50] Nevertheless, Bush has set a target of replacing 15% of domestic gasoline use with bio-fuels over the next decade. Already this has led to a doubling of the price of corn—and a boon for agri-business.

But like a latter day Captain Wrongway Peachfuzz, the cartoon character who inevitably did the wrong thing and traveled in the wrong direction, Bush—and his class—insist on pursuing a course that inexorably will bring the planet to the point of calamity. Bechtel is the poster-child for state monopoly capitalism. It flourishes due to contracts tendered by governments, and over the years has seen its top executives, e.g. Caspar Weinberger and George Shultz, lead the Pentagon and the State Department. Now it is on a crusade to own and operate water systems worldwide—a maneuver that led directly to an uprising in Bolivia.[51]

Privatization will lead to higher prices and more misery for the poor and the working class as a whole. A large share of the world's 852 million hungry people live on land with soils worn thin by erosion; the thin layer of topsoil that covers the planet's land surface is the foundation of civilization—and it is disappearing, which suggests that civilization itself is crumbling. The Sahara Desert is slowly spreading southward. Dust storms are now commonplace. Those who recall the Dust Bowl in Kansas and Oklahoma in the 1930s, which gave rise to John Steinbeck's classic *Grapes of Wrath*, have an inkling of what is befalling Africa.[52]

Meanwhile Monsanto, the U.S. based transnational corporation, is seeking to capitalize upon this global crisis that portends extinction of species by developing genetically modified organisms—particularly crops—and claiming patent rights on rice that, for example, has been grown in India for generations.[53]

U.S. imperialism historically has been indifferent to the fragility of the environment. Recall the Pentagon's lavish use of Agent Orange during the genocidal war against Vietnam. During this conflict about 12 million gallons of this defoliant were sprayed upon this Southeast Asian nation. It was intended to kill plants and strip leaves from trees in an effort to deprive the enemy of cover. It was little more than eco-cide, the intentional murder of the environment. It also murdered countless Vietnamese while leaving others with birth defects and other maladies.[54]

Thus, U.S. imperialism views itself as unbound by the financial, legal and environmental strictures that govern the international community as a whole. More specifically, U.S. imperialism stands decidedly to the right of the world. Rather than adapt to the world it seeks to forcefully impose its diktat and its narrow policies of deregulation and privatization. But the problem is that U.S. imperialism is in relative decline, as powers like China are rising. The tactless and indelicate policies of U.S. imperialism have driven China closer to Russia, and other nations are rapidly following their proclaimed attempt to construct a "multi-polar world and a new international order," as they put it in their important joint statement of 2 July 2005. They demanded that the UN play a "leading role in international affairs" and not self-proclaimed superpowers. They called for "the entry into force of the Comprehensive Nuclear Test Ban Treaty" and other pacts e.g. the "the Treaty on the Nonproliferation of Nuclear Weapons, the Convention on the Prohibition of Biological Weapons, and the Convention on the Prohibition of Chemical Weapons," not to mention the "peaceful use of outer space." Above all, they insisted upon "the principles of mutual respect for each other's sovereignty and territorial integrity, mutual non-aggression, non-interference in each other's internal affairs, equality, mutual benefit, and peaceful coexistence." [55]

Beijing and Moscow have tossed a gauntlet of peace before U.S. imperialism but it will be up to anti-imperialists—particularly in the U.S. itself—to make sure that this peaceful gesture is not ignored.

8: Future Wars? Fighting Back!

It sounds like bad science fiction—but, sadly, it is all too real.

Rapacious ruling class trashes Planet Earth, capitulates to global warming, then begins setting up in outer space for even more nefarious purposes.

Yet, this maddening scenario is occurring as I write.

One of the early acts of former Pentagon chief, Donald Rumsfeld, was a sweeping overhaul of space programs and the increase of the importance of the cosmos in strategic planning. A central purpose is Buck Rogers-style development of weapons for outer space. This includes lasers capable of shooting down ballistic missiles, and satellites designed to attack other satellites.[1] In short, U.S. imperialism is seeking to make the heavens a new arena of war. There is talk of a "Space Corps," just as there are amphibious Marines and discussion of a "Space Department." Official documents reference the 19th-century battle to control the oceans through the building of massive navies deemed mandatory for construction of empires, and how controlling outer space will be analogously necessary for hegemony in this century. "Missile Defense" or "Star Wars" is a foot in the door; that is, talk of defense—or hardening the shield—is like a good magician's trick designed to deflect attention away from what is really at stake: sharpening the sword of offensive weapons in space.

One of the last acts of the outgoing Clinton Administration in December 2000 was accelerating development of a Space-Based Laser, a joint project of TRW, Boeing and Lockheed Martin. Billions of dollars have been allocated for this hare-brained scheme. It is not enough for U.S. imperialism to have nuclear submarines underwater and long-range nuclear missiles on land, long-range nuclear bombers in the air and nuclear armed battleships on the water—no, that is not enough. Now there must be nuclear weapons in the heavens, perhaps on another planet.

An alarmed international community has not been quiescent as this rank lunacy has proceeded. In November 2000, as the *Bush v. Gore* case was winding catastrophically through the courts, a vote was held at the UN on a resolution calling for the "Prevention of an Arms Race in Outer

Space." It sought to reaffirm the Outer Space Treaty of 1967, the fundamental international law on this topic, and particularly its key provision that space be used for "peaceful purposes." In the event, some 163 nations voted affirmatively, but a cagey U.S. imperialism—an original mover of this important treaty—abstained. Instead, Washington power-brokers began to wax crazily about how it is the "manifest destiny" of U.S. imperialism to conquer the heavens just like their forefathers conquered the continent. Naturally, Moscow—which pioneered in sending a satellite into space in October, 1957, and continues to be a target of Washington's bellicosity—has been in the forefront of those taking exception to these plots.[2]

The passage of time has not induced sobriety in conservative hawks. In August 2004, the Pentagon articulated an actual "Counterspace Operations Doctrine," designed as the route through which Washington attains hegemony in the heavens. Then in March 2005, Secretary Rumsfeld signed a new National Defense Strategy paper that said the use of space "enables us to project power anywhere in the world from secure bases of operations." These are not just words. The Pentagon is developing a suborbital space capsule that could hit targets anywhere in the world within two hours of being launched from U.S. bases. Washington is moving toward a pre-emptive strategy for space, not unlike the disastrous pre-emptive war that is presently draining blood and treasure in Iraq. But like a punch-drunk boxer, U.S. imperialism seems incapable of thinking clearly and drawing the appropriate lessons from transforming defeats, e.g. what is now occurring in the former Mesopotamia. Ambassador Hu Xiaodi of China, a specialist in this realm, has warned Washington repeatedly that it is wandering down a perilous road—thus far, to no avail.[3] Moscow has issued similar warnings.[4]

Quite naturally—and bizarrely—the hawkish press has pointed to Hu Xiaodi's warnings as evidence of Beijing's bad intentions. According to the *Washington Times*, it is China that is "placing nuclear weapons in space."[5] "China Destroys Satellite in Test" was the blaring headline in the 19 January 2007 *New York Times*. More than most, Beijing is all too aware of the perfidy of U.S. imperialism, and is well-advised not to be outflanked in the heavens. But actually China's emphasis in space can be seen in its effort to launch a communications satellite for Nigeria, and developing an earth observation satellite system with Bangladesh, Indonesia, Iran, Mongolia, Pakistan, Peru and Thailand. A state-owned aerospace company, Great Wall Industry Corporation, will monitor the Nigerian satellite—called the Nigcomsat-1—from a ground station in northwestern China. It will also train Nigerian engineers to operate a tracking station in Abuja.[6]

Obviously, Washington would be well advised to follow such a space policy with an emphasis on mutual benefit for all humankind but, alas, that is akin to requesting demurely that the hyena change its behavior. The National Space Policy signed by Bush the Lesser in the Fall of 2006 envisions U.S. space diplomacy as basically persuading other nations to see things like Washington does. Of course, private enterprise is allocated a pre-eminent role (space warriors should not be deprived of their Starbucks coffee on Mars). Still, U.S. imperialism refuses adamantly to enter negotiations or even discussions on the delicate matter of space warfare. Despite this chilling reticence, the Pentagon has preferred to focus on the allegation made by National Reconnaissance Office Director, Donald M. Kerr, that a U.S. satellite had been "painted" or illuminated, by a laser in China, possibly to disrupt its functioning.[7]

Washington may think it has placed China on the back foot, not only because of its bluster and madcap spending on space warfare, but also because Japan has been encouraged to do the same, as part of what is seen as an anti-Beijing pincers maneuver. Yet *China Daily* reported blandly that Tokyo, fresh from its first satellite launch since a 2003 failure, announced grander plans, including putting a manned station on the moon in 2025. Japan, which has specialized in developing sophisticated robots, first plans to place one of these sophisticated mechanical devices on the moon. After noting Bush's announcement of a U.S.-manned mission to Mars by 2020, it was announced coolly that Beijing plans to land a spacecraft on the moon by 2010.[8]

For those who suspect that the insane dash for domination of U.S. imperialism knows no bounds, take heart: you very well may be correct. Since 1980, Washington—overtly or covertly—has been involved in military actions in Grenada, Libya, Nicaragua, Panama, Iraq, Afghanistan, El Salvador, Haiti, Somalia, Yugoslavia, Liberia, Sudan, the Philippines, Colombia, Haiti (once more), Afghanistan (again), Iraq (once more)—and let's not even count the support for various "insurgencies" in Mozambique, Angola and elsewhere. This bloody experience has given Washington a bunch of bright ideas about how best to end life. Currently the Air Force Research Laboratory has been conducting research on the effects of "directed energy technologies" on people and animals. One critical area involved identifying "biological tissue thresholds (minimum visible lesion) and damage mechanisms from laser and non-laser sources." Translation? How much pain can be inflicted without leaving those bothersome telltale thermal burns? The threshold of pain is a rich area of study for the mad scientists of U.S. imperialism—the problem thus far is that we progressives have not made such madness painful for them to engage in.

Thus, research has continued apace on the so-called Active Denial

System or "painful energy beam" weapon; of course, Washington war-mongers salivate at the mention of the Pulsed Energy Projectiles, which inflicts pain so horrific that it is painful to even read about. In sum, to coin a phrase that an honest Pentagon might, these are Mobile Torture Devices (MTDs). PEPs are designed to punish nerve cells, causing excruciating pain that can be inflicted from up to 2 miles away from the victim. And, yes, Pentagon contractors are elbowing one another aside in order to grab these lucrative assignments.[9]

Just like water-boarding—the signature torture of the Bush lea-guers—which makes the victim feel like he's drowning, the Active Denial System makes the victim feel like he or she is on fire. Raytheon is the proud papa of this form of torture.[10] But their partners in crime have little reason to be envious. Lockheed Martin, which runs the Sandia nuclear weapons engineering laboratory in New Mexico, and builds Trident sub-marine-launched ballistic missiles, has been profiting quite nicely, thank you, from the White House's increased investment in the development and deployment of ever newer nukes. The Big Four Merchants of Death—Lockheed Martin, Boeing, TRW and, of course, Raytheon—will reap bil-lions of dollars in taxpayer funds to build the Bush version of Star Wars, which could, equal more than a quarter of a trillion dollars over the next decade.[11]

But just like Microsoft scooped IBM, and Google may do the same to the Seattle leviathan, the Big Four are now quaking in their hand-sewn Gucci loafers at the prospect that Big Pharma may shovel into its pockets even more filthy lucre than themselves in coming years. To some in Washington, the Big Four are "old school," very 1999 in thinking, while the hip money is banking on Chemical and Biological Warfare.

Yes, there is that small matter of the Chemical Weapons Convention and an entire body of well-developed law on this matter. But the CWC has an exemption for domestic law enforcement, so-called "riot control," such as was seen in Los Angeles in 1965 and 1992, and Newark and Detroit in 1967. Certain governments made a loophole for domestic purposes that they now plan to use—presumably—for external purposes. But the use of tear gas, which was concentrating the minds of many negotiating the CWC, is child's play compared to what's in store for those who dare to resist the iron fist of U.S. imperialism. Thus, molecules can now be re-engineered to target bio-regulation processes including neurological func-tions and cardiovascular processes. Already it has been reported that strapped, over-burdened U.S. forces in Iraq have been fed drugs to height-en alertness. We may soon see troops charge into battle with chemically heightened aggression, as well as resistance to fear, pain and fatigue. We may soon see troops charge into battle high on drugs that reduce or obliterate feelings of guilt or even post-traumatic stress. After all, by a factor of five, more soldiers suffer mental rather than physical wounds in war.

Actually it was in 1999 that the European Parliament, sensing the pharmacological turn, called for a global ban on all research and development, whether military or civilian, which seeks to apply knowledge of the chemical, electrical, sound vibration or other functioning of the human brain to the development of weapons which might enable any form of manipulation of human beings. U.S. imperialism yawned as it laughed at the very idea of forswearing any kind of weapons research. Military researchers continue to investigate weapons that can induce liver cancer, for example. Weapons are being designed to carry drugs to targets; flight-stabilized syringes, mortar bombs for dispersing chemical agents; modified paint-ball guns; micro-encapsulated pellets which release an agent when stepped on; and unmanned area vehicles. Ever more fiendish experiments have been conducted to "enhance" Tasers, which already have wreaked havoc on urban populations in the U.S.[12]

Of course, the next step in this diabolical planning is to trigger earthquakes, induce hurricanes and tsunamis, and generate—quite literally—the proverbial "fog of war." [13] Why stop there? Why not "melanin bombs" and other "racial weapons" ? Why not, indeed. It is well known that there were previously efforts in the U.S. to tailor the Valley Fever virus to the perceived uniqueness of the African-American population who were thought to be ten times as likely to perish from this illness as their Euro-American counterparts. The ugly apartheid authorities could have taught their U.S. cousins—and most likely did—a thing or three about this route to genocide.[14]

Tragically, in seeking to prepare dangerous toxins to subdue enemies near and far, U.S. imperialism may wind up extinguishing itself. Since 2003 research funding for the National Institute of Allergy and Infectious Diseases, which administers so-called "bio-defense" spending, has leapt from $187 million to $1.6 billion. Unsurprisingly, the number of accidents involving dangerous microbes has rocketed simultaneously, including multiple exposures of live anthrax bacteria.[15] Of potentially disastrous consequence was the Summer 2007 incident, when the Air Force mistakenly flew six nuclear bombs on a B-52 bomber from North Dakota to Louisiana in violation of military guidelines. The U.S.—and not just U.S. imperialism—could have been wiped out in one stroke if the plane had crashed. Congressman Edward Markey said this incident had "frightening implications." [16]

But as the great Bertolt Brecht once suggested, it is one thing to cook up ever more monstrous means of murder—it is quite another to find those willing to execute these plans (even if fed with mind-altering drugs).

Conservative hawks have not left this to chance. Today, Regent University, the flagship university of the openly and flagrantly theocratic wing of the GOP, which boosted Bush to power, has 150 alumni toiling away in the bowels of his regime.[17] Though Washington has been vociferously hostile to the notion of affirmative action—there are exceptions. Consider the recruitment policies for the CIA, for example. Before leaving in disgrace, former Director George Tenet appointed an African-American, Donald R. Cryer, as his Special Assistant for Diversity. Perhaps the appropriately named Mr. Cryer can aid in purging from the memories of all too many African-Americans the unforgettable story of how CIA policy in Central America helped to fuel a crack cocaine epidemic in South Los Angeles, then nationally.[18]

Perhaps, further, it reflects the abject desperation of a U.S. imperialism grounded in white supremacy that they now feel compelled to recruit the prime victims of this system to defend it, not unlike the Confederate States of America seeking to recruit enslaved Africans for their putrid cause in the dying days of the Civil War.

Unfortunately, this is an appropriate analogy, for despite the dogged devastation that has been visited upon African-Americans most notably in recent years, somehow the illusion persists that—as in an unrealistic Hollywood tearjerker—the aggrieved Negro will ride to the rescue once more of Ol' Massa. (Sorry, I'm not sure how to break this to you except to say, it just ain't happening).

In mid-2007 as the smell of death in Iraq and Afghanistan could almost be detected in Harlem, a stunned reporter for the Associated Press revealed that "the number of blacks joining the military has plunged by more than one-third" since just after 9/11, when patriotic spirit was thought by the naïve to have attained stratospheric levels. One reason: "relatives of potential recruits increasingly discourage them from signing up." The decline is ecumenical, covering all four services (and when the "Space Corps" is up and running, that will mean a decline in five). According to Pentagon data, "there were nearly 51,500 new black recruits for active duty and reserves in 2001." However, that lofty number plummeted precipitously to less than 32,000 in 2006, a 38 percent decline. When only active duty troops are counted, the number of black recruits went from more than 31,000 in 2002 to about 23,600 in 2006, almost one-quarter fewer." The decline has been particularly stark for the Army, who along with Marines, are most decisively in harm's way.[19]

Now the Pentagon is desperate, with plans for developing robot troops in research over-drive as the nation's youth—even faced with parlous economic conditions at home—are increasingly unwilling to risk their lives for lost causes. This has been readily apparent for some time.

In early 2005, as the wars were grinding down U.S. troops like so much hamburger meat at an abattoir, the Marines missed their monthly recruiting goals for the first time in a decade; the Army and National Guard similarly fell short. The military now acknowledges that the Coalition Against Militarism in Schools, antiwar activists comprised primarily of high school teachers—e.g. in one of their bastions: Los Angeles—is a major reason why students run in the other direction when the men in uniform arrive.[20]

An occupation requires "boots on the ground" soldiers, but if they are not be found the mission withers—particularly when the population to be occupied is unfriendly to the troops. The shortfall in recruiting, driven in no small part by the "strike" of youthful African-Americans, who would rather fight for Justice in Jena, Louisiana, than Injustice in Iraq, has meant that the U.S. military is on the verge of snapping. This is the grim conclusion drawn by the senior GOP Senator from Indiana, Richard Lugar. He laments that the Army is recruiting more felons, and has relaxed age and weight standards—though as of yet there is no indication that criteria have melted to the point where "chicken hawks" like Dick Cheney and George Will and Rush Limbaugh will finally get the opportunity to serve their nation in uniform, something they have been energetic in bestowing upon so many others.[21]

The Pentagon has gotten so desperate that it has been reduced to partnering with "Labor Ready," a provider of temporary jobs for mostly "unskilled" workers; in turn, the low wage champion that is Labor Ready is targeting the spouses of National Guardsmen and Guardsmen themselves felled by unemployment.[22]

One must wonder on what universe Pentagon planners reside (or perhaps they dipped prematurely into a vat of mind-altering drugs), for if they were paying attention they would know that Black America is concerned alright about the Gulf—the Gulf Coast of the U.S. and the Bush regime's foot-dragging approach to rebuilding New Orleans in particular, and guaranteeing the right of return for those driven out.

This in itself would be enough to drive Black America and its many allies into an angry stupor, but combined with the arrogance of U.S. imperialism, which has refused to accept generous offers from abroad for Gulf Coast relief, only deepens the profundity of the fury. Bangladesh, Pakistan, Peru, Holland, Denmark, Sweden and many more nations offered electric generators and baby formula, doctors and beddings, and more. But it was refused though many were suffering.[23]

Socialist Cuba, as is typical of this heroic nation, offered to send 1600 battle-tested physicians. Even Senator Mel Martinez of Florida, otherwise a conservative hawk, thought that aid should be accepted from his former homeland: Bush kept his head buried ostrich-like in the sands—of Iraq.[24] As criminally neglected corpses continued to float in the fetid waters of New Orleans, and hungry and thirsty African-Americans were deposited like cattle and herded into sports arenas, Cuba's National Assembly offered material solidarity.[25] Washington refused—and Black America steamed. Unsurprisingly, approximately two years later, tens of thousands of African-Americans were marching in Louisiana—Jena, in this instance—for justice.

African-Americans can also be found in the front ranks of those in organized labor on the march. There has been a noticeable turnabout in unions generally, particularly if it is recalled that on the afternoon of 8 May 1970, some 200 construction workers attacked a Wall Street rally against the war in Vietnam. The demented, demagogic, anti-Semitic and racist U.S. President, Richard M. Nixon, was so joyful about this disastrous turn of events that he named the New York City building trades leader, Peter Brennan, who egged on the workers, as his Secretary of Labor. As the burly, balding, cigar-chomping, and hysterically anti-Communist AFL-CIO union chief, George Meany, was on the verge of death in 1980, with ample opportunity to reconsider—minimally—the cost and need of over 50,000 U.S. deaths in Indo-China and millions more of indigenes, he told an interviewer in an unusual burst of acuity, "If I had known then what I know now, I would have acted differently about the war."

To the credit of labor, in confronting the invasion of Iraq—from the beginning of this conflict in Spring of 2003—unions have followed in the footsteps of the later version of Meany and not Brennan. Even before this disaster erupted, labor bluntly announced that the billions of dollars needed for this catastrophe, would come from "schools, hospitals, housing and social security." The war drive, it was stated forthrightly in early 2003, was already serving as a "pretext for attacks on labor, civil, immigrant and human rights at home," as well as a "distraction for the sinking economy, corporate corruption and layoffs."

This illuminating resolution was adopted at a January 2003 conference in Chicago. The site of this gathering—the nation's largest Teamsters trucking local—was an indication that anti-war sentiment had spread widely among organized labor. Signing this document were national leaders of postal workers, as well as the central labor councils of Los Angeles, Philadelphia, Cleveland, Sacramento—and many more. Local unions representing painters, carpenters, plumbers, teachers, and hotel and auto workers also signed. In New York, the vanguard of labor, the health and hospital workers union, 1199 of the Service Employees International Union, which has given office space to anti-war protest organizers, bought radio time to advertise a massive rally that galvanized peace forces.[26]

This powerful peace sentiment in the House of Labor has not abated. During the Summer of 2007, Leo Gerard, President of the United Steel Workers (which also represents oil workers), sent a similarly powerful message to Congressional and Senatorial leaders. Sailing into the wind of Washington's—present—dominant ideology, Gerard insisted that "Iraq's oil is a national resource that should not be privatized," and demanded a ceasefire in the ongoing war against Iraqi labor.[27]

Local, state and national organizations representing 13 million workers around the nation adopted resolutions criticizing the impending war—before it occurred. Yes, back then there was not unanimity of opinion about the war. There was an ill-fated Committee for the Liberation of Iraq that attracted some support from leaders of the Teamsters but, in the context of what is growing and what is decaying, this trend was certainly in the latter camp.[28]

African-American women—who probably are the most significant mass left sector in the electorate—also have been an important part of this labor upsurge. This reflects a global trend in that the International Confederation of Free Trade Unions notes that 40% of its 156 million membership are women, which reflects the global workforce. Black women—and women globally—have questioned pointedly and passionately why taxpayer dollars are going for war and not for health care, child care, human needs.[29]

Labor has also been in the vanguard of the battle against climate change. In the Spring of 2007 in New York City, the North American Assembly on Climate Crisis was held, sponsored by hemispheric unions, including the U.S., Canada, Mexico and the Caribbean, along with 50 other unionists from other regions of the world. This Assembly was one of a series of global gatherings that began with the First Global Trade Union Assembly on Labour and the Environment in Nairobi in January 2006. In April 2006 Brazil hosted the first ever Trade Union Regional Conference on Labour and the Environment for unions in Latin America and in July 2006 another Regional Conference took place, this time in Johannesburg, South Africa.

What is remarkable about these confabs—particularly the one in New York—is the clarity that shines through what was said. "Unions have long maintained," it was announced boldly, "that climate stabilization can only be accomplished if economic and social life is structured around the notion of sustainable development and fair trade," both of which presuppose "worker participation in important decisions affecting the workplace and economic life in general." A more potent challenge to "cowboy capitalism," which is grounded in unsustainable development and unfair trade, can hardly be imagined. Further, these workers, "along with unions around the world," chose to "embrace the concept of 'just transition' whereby no worker should suffer economic hardship or insecurity as a result of the changes required to address climate crisis or other environmental challenges." Demanded were "new and well paying 'green' jobs in renewable energy, the construction trades, public transportation, sustainable farming and much-needed manufacturing."

To effectuate this ambitious agenda, these workers cried out for "the greatest possible trade union unity and coordinated practical action." Similarly, "'blue-green' alliances...between unions, environmental and community organizations must be grounded in the understanding that the fate of workers, communities and the biosphere ae inseparable from each other." [30]

There is substantial reason to believe that these farsighted words will reach fruition. To understand why, look no further than the nation's second largest city: Los Angeles. Once renowned as a citadel of reaction and anti-union fervor, it has become renowned in recent years as the headquarters of the nation's fastest growing and most effective labor movement, a trailblazing trend that is inseparable from the demographic reality that this city also has the most diverse agglomeration of Latino workers in the hemisphere. Those of Mexican origin are front and center of course, but L.A. also features a hardy corps of workers with far-reaching experiences in uncivil conflicts in El Salvador and Guatemala as well. This trans-national experience gives these workers and their unions a powerful asset when they are compelled to confront capital. Thus, in 1999, more workers joined unions in L.A.—91,000—than in any metropolis since Walter Reuther organized the auto workers in 1930s Detroit. Here one espies the inescapable contradictions that have ensnared U.S. imperialism—brutal wars in Central America fed a migration to L.A. that has transformed this megalopolis to labor's advantage. A telling point is that at that historic moment of union membership upsurge, the Political Director of L.A. Labor was Fabian Núñez—who now holds the second most powerful post in the state: Speaker of the Assembly, where he routinely bests the intellectually challenged Governor Arnold Schwarznegger.[31]

But as heartening as the news is from L.A.—news that spells ill for the fortunes of U.S. imperialism—perhaps more heartening is the news from around the globe. Just before 9/11, General Motors Europe was obliged to back down from plans to force layoffs of thousands of workers and close one of 13 European plants; this occurred as 12,500 workers at Volkswagen's plant in Puebla, Mexico, went on strike, demanding a 21% pay increase, and 4000 workers were striking for higher wages at a plant then controlled by DaimlerChrysler in South Africa.[32]

Africa, which has been the heart and soul of the pattern-setting Non-Aligned Movement and the UN General Assembly, also has been in the forefront of the gathering trend of cross-border labor solidarity, so as to better confront imperialism. In January 2000 the Nigeria Labour Congress and the Congress of South African Trade Unions agreed to cooperate. Putting it pithily was NLC President Adams Oshiomhole who told those assembled that the alliance with COSATU was necessary, considering that governments and businesses "with all their enormous resources, are moving beyond their national boundaries, trying strategic alliances and relations to achieve their respective objectives." [33]

Interestingly enough, this battle between capital and labor led to an unprecedented lobbyist journey to Washington by Chinese scholar and labor-law expert Lie Cheng, who sought to drum up support from U.S. legislators and labor leaders for a law that is pending—not before the U.S. Congress—but before the National People's Congress in Beijing. On one side are Wal-Mart, Google, GE and other behemoths who have been aggressively lobbying to limit new rights for Chinese workers. Across the barricades are pro-worker-rights forces in China backed by labor, human rights and political forces in the U.S. and around the world.[34] Of course, progressive labor on this side of the Pacific have been active in their solidarity with their Chinese counterparts.

This is where U.S. labor needs to be, for the collapse of the Soviet Union has created a new global dispensation that capital finds quite congenial. The economist, Richard Freeman, argues that there has been an effective doubling of the global labor force (i.e. workers producing for international markets) over the past decade and a half, through the entry of Chinese, Indian, Russian and other workers into the global economy. The effective supply of capital, he says, has virtually remained unchanged—thus contributing to a declining share of labor's share of the returns from production. As China and India graduate more engineers and technical workers, he suggests, under prevailing norms and conditions, they will be thrust into competition with their counterparts in North America.[35] The trick is to alter radically the "prevailing norms and conditions" through such time-tested means as global labor solidarity that progressively shrinks the prerogatives of capital.

Ironically, labor—in fact, all of us—have much to learn in this regard from the original inhabitants of this land: Native Americans. It was in 1923 that Chief Deskaheh of the Cayuga people—now occupied by Cornell University and its environs—traveled to Geneva to address the League of Nations about the right of his people to live freely on their lands, practice their own religion and follow their own laws. The door was shut in his face by what he termed "cruel indifference." But on 13 September 2007, the U.N. General Assembly adopted the historic Declaration on the Rights of Indigenous Peoples: 143 nations voted in favor, 11 abstained. And 4 dissented: the U.S., Canada, Australia and New Zealand, the leading exemplars of settler colonialism and the nations that will be compelled in the near future to alter radically their internal situations, not least due to global pressure and solidarity. The "right to restitution" is a key principle of this UN Declaration, which neatly parallels the "right to reparations" now being demanded by African-Americans.[36] Labor has to realize that their own battle for a greater share of the national income will be enhanced to the extent these struggles meet with success, just as labor would be well-advised to step up its engagement with the international community.

Washington is now obliged to report to the U.N. about its responsibilities concerning the elimination of racial discrimination. Because of adroit lobbying by the Western Shoshone people of the Great Basin (now known as Nevada), the U.N. has called on the federal government to respect and protect the rights of this heroic though embattled people. Further, the UN has demanded that the US not only respect treaties signed with the indigenes but, further, they should be construed in a way that are favorable "for Indian interests." [37]

Kara Briggs of the American Indian Policy and Media Initiative spoke for many when she asserted in thunderstruck terms, "I can't help but wonder how the world would be different if 400 years ago, we, the colonized of the world, had this central gathering place to confer about atrocities and organize a worldwide resistance." [38] But just as global pressure generated by the likes of the sophisticated Communist attorney, William Patterson and his fellow African-American activist, Paul Robeson, led to charging Washington with genocide against African-Americans in various international fora, thereby hastening the demise of formal Jim Crow, the original inhabitants of this continent are now following in these footsteps with resultant parallel consequences.[39]

Fortunately, the objective conditions needed for indigenous success are more favorable today in an era of the relative decline of U.S. imperialism, as opposed to 1950 when Patterson and Robeson were crusading. This reality became clear in March 2007, when a colorful and historic gathering took place in Guatemala, the III Continental Summit of Indigenous Nations and Pueblos of Abya Yala . Present were about 2800 indigenous peoples from some 24 nations, including some 125 Aymara representatives who arrived in their own plane—courtesy of heroic Bolivian President, Evo Morales. Western Shoshone representatives arrived—and were admitted—with the passports of their own nations, not that of the U.S. This was precedent shattering, but not unusual, in that Hopi representatives have traveled globally for some time bereft of documents from Washington, but armed with documents of their nation.[40] In Hawaii, indigenes have organized marches for sovereignty featuring tens of thousands, in an explicit rebuke to the illegal machinations of the 1890s that led to their nation being swallowed by a nascent U.S. imperialism.[41]

Human rights advocates in the U.S. have taken a cue from the indigenes and in an implicit thumbing of the nose at domestic courts that have been captured and occupied by conservative hawks, have begun to turn increasingly to international bodies for redress. Victims of torture by police authorities have demanded that the U.S. live up to its obligation under various international conventions and treaties,[42] while Amnesty International has traveled to Geneva in order to charge U.S. police with the illegal use of pepper spray, tear gas and electric-shock devices in blatant violation of global norms.[43] The government of Mexico has intervened aggressively on behalf of its nationals that are incarcerated in the dank dungeons in the U.S. that are called prisons. Specifically, it sued in the World Court to force local U.S. authorities to allow Mexican diplomats to have access to their nationals facing conviction for capital crimes. After first dismissing the very thought of this alleged interference in the U.S., the Bush regime—as a direct reflection of the relative decline of U.S. imperialism—chose to acquiesce and is now seeking to compel a recalcitrant Texas to see things its way.[44]

All of these militant actions are part of a developing "all-peoples global front" against U.S. imperialism, a strategic imperative for our times.

Appropriately, this trend has reached its efflorescence in Puerto Rico, where in a typical manifestation, masses gathered in the Plaza of the Revolution in Lares, to commemorate the 139th anniversary of the island's rebellion against Spanish rule. But on 23 September 2007, the accent was on protest against another kind of foreign rule—that of U.S. imperialism.

And the entire island of Puerto Rico was riveted.

INTRODUCTION

1. *Washington Post*, 18 August 2007.

2. *St. Louis Post-Dispatch*, 14 March 2005.

3. *Ibid.*, 4 June 2007.

4. anc.org.za/ancdocs/anctoday/2001/at36.htm, 28 September-4 October 2001.

5. See e.g. Philip Bonosky, *Washington's Secret War Against Afghanistan*, New York: International Publishers, 1985.

6. *Le Nouvel Observateur* (France), 15-21 January 1998.

7. blogs/abcnews.com/theblotter/2007/04/abc_news_exclus.html, 3 April 2007.

8. *The Independent* (London), 24 February 2005.

9. *San Francisco Chronicle*, 22 February 2002.

10. *Boston Globe*, 1 August 2007.

11. *San Bernandino County Sun*, 15 February 2007.

12. *Los Angeles Times*, 14 May 2007.

13. tomdispatch.com/post/174830, 20 August 2007.

14. *Asia Times*, 28 January 2006 (atimes.com).

15. *Financial Times*, 15 January 2006.

16. *Reuters*, 13 February 2006.

17. *Financial Times*, 30 April 2007.

18. *Ibid*, 26 April 2007.

19. *Ibid*, 2 August 2007.

20. *Los Angeles Times*, 25 May 2007.

21. *Financial Times*, 26 January 2007.

22. *New York Times*, 17 August 2007.

23. *New York Times*, 29 August 2007.

24. *New York Times*, 28 August 2006.

25. *New York Times*, 21 August 2007.

26. See e.g. Gerald Horne, *Black and Red: W.E.B. Du Bois and the Afro-American Response to the Cold War, 1944-1963*, Albany: State University of New York Press, 1986; Gerald Horne, *Black Liberation/Red Scare: Ben Davis and the Communist Party*, Newark University of Delaware Press, 1994.

27. *New York Times*, 1 February 2007.

28. *Houston Chronicle*, 22 August 2007.

29. *Financial Times*, 10 July 2007.

30. *Financial Times*, 1 February 2007.

31. *Washington Post*, 9 October 2005.

32. *Houston Chronicle*, 22 August 2007.

33. *Granma*, 22 December 1999.

34. Sara Bongiorni, *A Year Without 'Made in China': One Family's True Life Adventure in the Global Economy*, New York: Wiley, 2007.

35. *Financial Times*, 5 June 2007.

36. *Financial Times*, 29 May 2007.

37. *New York Times*, 18 April 2007.

38. *Washington Post*, 10 April 2000.

39. *China Daily*, 23 March 2006.
40. *Daily Telegraph* [U.K.], 8 August 2007.
41. *Reuters*, 4 April 2006.
42. *New York Times*, 16 August 2007.
43. *Granma*, 24 June 2007.
44. *San Francisco Chronicle*, 14 April 2001.
45. *Forward*, 16 March 2007.
46. *Financial Times*, 29 March 2006.
47. *New York Times*, 11 June 2007.
48. *China Daily*, 3 March 2005.
49. *Financial Times*, 29-30 July 2006.
50. *Los Angeles Times*, 4 May 2007.
51. *Granma*, 5 September 2005.
52. politicalaffairs.net, 3 September 2005.
53. *Counterpunch*, 4 March 2003.
54. uslaboragainstwar.org, 24 February 2003.
55. *Christian Science Monitor*, 27 February 2003.
56. afterdowningstreet.org/node/25286, 31 July 2007.
57. *New York Times*, 20 May 2006.
58. *In These Times*, February 2007; Utne Reader, July-August 2007.
59. JoeSims@politicalaffairs.net to Gerald Horne, 4 August 2000 (in possession of author).

1: THE BUSINESS OF WAR

1. *Washington Times*, 31 October 2001.
2. *Washington Times*, 1 November 2001.
3. *Agence France Presse*, 7 October 2001.
4. H-DIPLO@H-NET.MSU.EDU, 23 August 2002.
5. *Los Angeles Times*, 29 September 2001.
6. See e.g. Gerald Horne, *Fire this Time: The Watts Uprising and the 1960s*, Charlottesville: University of Virginia Press, 1995.
7. Robert Dreyfuss, *Devil's Game: How the United States Helped Unleash Fundamentalist Islam*, New York: Metropolitan Books, 2005.
8. Gary Sick, *October Surprise: America's Hostages in Iran and the Election of Ronald Reagan*, New York: Times Books, 1991.
9. *Guardian* [U.K.], 23 October 2001.
10. *The Guardian* [UK], 10 September 2005.
11. *New York Sun*, 30 July 2007.
12. *Wall Street Journal*, 7 August 2007.
13. *Washington Post*, 6 August 2002.
14. *New York Times*, 27 July 2007.
15. *New York Times*, 15 December 2001.
16. *The Hindu* [India], 13 October 2001.
17. *Guardian* [UK], 23 October 2001.See also Ahmed Rashid, *Taliban: Militant Islam, Oil & Fundamentalism in Central Asia*, New Haven: Yale University Press, 2000.

18. Transcript, 8 January 2002, 7:34 AM, ET, cnn.com.

19. *Los Angeles Times*, 13 September 2007.

20. *Guardian* [UK], 28 August 2007.

21. *Le Monde Diplomatique*, March 2007.

22. tomdispatch.com/post/174810>, 16 June 2007.

23. *Los Angeles Times*, 1 July 2007.

24. *New York Times*, 5 March 2001.

25. *Los Angeles Times*, 10 January 2002.

26. *Business Week*, 23-28 August 2000.

27. *Washington Post*, 21 September 2005.

28. *San Francisco Chronicle*, 12 August 2007.

29. *Los Angeles Times*, 4 July 2007.

30. *New York Times*, 3 October 2007.

2: THE AGONY OF WAR

1. unitedforpeace.org/downloads/peoplesreport.pdf, 10 September 2007.

2. *Guardian*, [UK] 30 July 2007.

3. *Washington Times*, 20 January 2006.

4. gulflink.osd.mil.See also *The Progressive*, September 2001.

5. *Washington Post*, 6 July 2001.

6. *Hartford Courant*, 10 January 1999.

7. *Guardian* [UK], 24 April 2007.

8. *New York Times*, 28 February 2007. See also appealforredress.org.

9. *Ibid.*, 23 March 2007.

10. *El Paso Times*, 14 September 2007.

11. *Washington Post*, 18 August 2007.

12. *New York Amsterdam News*, 10-16 November 2006.

13. *In These Times*, June 2007.

14. *In These Times*, August 2007.

15. *Toronto Star*, 17 August 2007.

16. *Los Angeles Times*, 26 May 2007.

17. *Ibid., Times*, 5 January 2007.

18. nsnetwork.org, 2 May 2007.

19. splcenter.org/intel/news/item, 7 July 2006.

20. John J. Mearsheimer and Stephen Walt, *The Israel Lobby and U.S. Foreign Policy*, New York: Farrar, Straus & Giroux, 2007.

21. *Forward*, 21 September 2007.

22. *Washington Post*, 7 May 2001.

23. *Los Angeles Times*, 1 October 2006.

24. *Insight*, 22-28 August 2006.

25. *Washington Post*, 11 September 2004.

26. *Ibid.*, 18 May 2007.

27. *Associated Press*, 19 January 2007.

28. *Guardian,* 13 June 2007.

29. *Washington Times*, 2 July 2002.

30. *Financial Times*, 20-21 May 2006.

31. *Financial Times*, 22 June 2007.

32. *Reuters*, 13 February 2006.

33. Trita Parsi, *Treacherous Alliance: The Secret Dealings of Israel, Iran and the United States*, New Haven: Yale University Press, 2007.

34. *Los Angeles Times*, 30 December 2006.

35. *Financial Times*, 3 August 2007.

36. *Final Call*, 29 May 2007.

37. *Forward*, 25 May 2007.

38. *Los Angeles Times*, 23 April 2006.

39. *The American Prospect*, 6 July 2007.

40. uslaboragainstwar.org, 4 August 2007.

41. tomdispatch, 11 July 2007.

3: CHINA'S PEACEFUL RISE/U.S. IMPERIALISM'S INEXORABLE DECLINE

1. Gerald Horne, "Rethinking the History and Future of the Communist Party," politicalaffairs.net, March 2007.

2. *Los Angeles Times*, 1 September 2007.

3. *Asia Times*, 3 October 2006.

4. *Xinhua* [China], 31 October 2005.

5. *New York Times*, 28 May 2001.

6. *South China Morning Post*, 6 April 2001.

7. *New York Times*, 4 July 2007.

8. *Financial Times*, 6 February 2007.

9. *Asia Times*, 4 April 2007.

10. *Business Week*, 16 April 2007.

11. *Financial Times*, 9 February 2007.

12. *Financial Times*, 19 March 2007.

13. *Wall Street Journal*, 4 May 2006.

14. *Business Day*, 30 March 2006.

15. *Asia Times*, 3 October 2006.

16. *Financial Times*, 26-27 May 2007.

17. *Financial Times*, 25 January 2007.

18. *Prensa Latina* [Cuba], 24 August 2007.

19. *Asia Times*, 14 December 2005.

20. *Financial Times*, 3-4 February 2007.

21. *New York Times*, 25 May 2001.

22. Jean Pfaelzer, *Driven Out: The Forgotten War Against Chinese Americans*, New York: Random House, 2007.

23. *Financial Times*, 30 August 2006.

24. *Financial Times*, 16 June 2006.

25. *Financial Times*, 13 March 2007.

26. *Asia Times*, 15 December 2005.

27. *Ibid.*, 30 April 2006.

28. *Financial Times*, 9 February 2007.

29. *Japan Times* [Tokyo], 3 June 2001.

30. *New York Times*, 16 September 2007.

31. *Ibid.*, 6 March 2001.

32. Amy Chua, *World on Fire: How Exporting Free Market Democracy Breeds Ethnic Hatred and Global Instability*, New York: Anchor, 2004.

33. *China Daily*, 29 July 2005.

34. *Los Angeles Times*, 6 June 2007.

35. Marion V. Creekmore, *A Moment of Crisis: Jimmy Carter, the Power of a Peacemaker and North Korea's Nuclear Ambitions*, New York: Public Affairs, 2007; *New York Review of Books*, 1 March 2007.

36. *Guardian*, [UK], 7 September 2007.

37. *Houston Chronicle*, 14 October 1999.

38. *South China Morning Post*, 27 November 2000.

39. *Los Angeles Times*, 25 August 2006.

40. *China Daily,* 21 December 2005.

41. *Business Week*, 11 June 2007.

42. *New York Times*, 4 April 2007.

43. *Ibid.,* 18 April 2007.

44. *Guardian* [UK], 30 March 2006.

45. *Financial Times*, 3 August 2007.

46. *Washington Post*, 13 July 2005.

47. *Washington Post*, 6 April 2001.

48. *Washington Post*, 18 April 2001.

49. *New York Times*, 6 April 2001.

50. *New York Times*, 3 June 2001.

51. *Financial Times*, 26-27 May 2007.

52. *Financial Times*, 25 May 2007.

53. *Financial Times*, 25 May 2007.

54. *Washington Times*, 16 May 2006.

55. *New York Times*, 13 June 2007.

56. *Washington Times*, 26 July 2005.

57. *Washington Post*, 22 August 2000.

58. *Financial Times*, 26 April 2007.

59. *Washington Times*, 2 August 2001.

60. Wen Ho Lee, *My Country Versus Me: The First-Hand Account by the Los Alamos Scientist who was Falsely Accused of Being a Spy*, New York: Hyperion, 2003.

61. *New York Times*, 20 January 2000.

62. salon.com, 6 June 2000.

63. *USA Today*, 23 July 2007.

64. *Ibid.,* 24 July 2007.

65. *Houston Chronicle*, 29 April 2007.

66. *Reuters*, 14 June 2001.

67. *Asia Times*, 17 April 2006.

68. *People's Weekly World*, 12-18 May 2007.

4: CUBA SI, YANQUI NO

1. *Granma* [Cuba], 1 April 2007.
2. *Washington Times*, 12 June 2001.
3. *Reuters*, 21 March 2006.
4. *Le Monde Diplomatique*, [France], August 2006.
5. Michael Moore to Secretary of the Treasury Henry Paulson, 11 May 2007, michaelmoore.com/words/message/index.php?id+207>.
6. yesmagazine.org/article.asp?ID=1733, 5 June 2007.
7. *New York Times*, 28 March 2001.
8. irinnews.org, 28 March 2001.
9. *InterPress Third World News Agency*, 30 April 2001.
10. *New York Times*, 27 May 2007.
11. *Los Angeles Times*, 18 February 2007.
12. *Granma* [Cuba], 11 February 2007.
13. *Los Angeles Times*, 24 December 2006.
14. *Wall Street Journal*, 13 January 2007.
15. *Granma* [Cuba], 5 August 2007.
16. *Los Angeles Times*, 14 July 2001.
17. *New York Times*, 3 February 2002.
18. *Chronicle of Higher Education*, 3 August 2007.
19. Ibid., Michael Moore to Secretary of the Treasury Henry Paulson, 11 May 2007.
20. *The Final Call*, 26 June 2007.
21. *People's Weekly World*, 5-11 May 2007.
22. *Jamaica Observer*, 13 September 2007.
23. *New York Times*, 24 August 2007.
24. *Miami Herald*, 25 September 2001.
25. *Los Angeles Times*, 20 April 2007.
26. *Granma* [Cuba], 20 May 2007.
27. *Chicago Tribune*, 19 August 2007.
28. *New York Times*, 13 December 2005.
29. *New York Times*, 28 March 2001.
30. *Washington Post*, 4 March 2005.
31. *Washington Times*, 17 April 2007.
32. *American Prospect*, 11 June 2007.
33. *Mother Jones*, 26 November 2001.
34. *Houston Chronicle*, 16 January 2007.
35. *Indian Country Today*, 6 June 2007.
36. *New York Times*, 18 January 2006.
37. *Los Angeles Times*, 30 April 2007.
38. See e.g. Gerald Horne, *Black and Brown: African-Americans and the Mexican Revolution, 1910-1920*, New York: New York University Press, 2005.
39. *USA Today*, 9 August 2007.
40. *Los Angeles Times*, 5 April 2007.
41. *Washington Post*, 28 February 2005.
42. *Miami Herald*, 12 August 2000.

43. *Guardian* [UK], 6 June 2001.

44. *Los Angeles Times*, 27 May 2007.

45. *Christian Science Monitor*, 28 November 2005.

46. *New York Times*, 1 October 2007.

47. *Los Angeles Times*, 25 April 2007.

48. *Los Angeles Times*, 15 January 2007.

49. *Granma* [Cuba], 13 May 2007.

50. *New York Amsterdam News*, 10-16 May 2007.

51. *Business Week*, 9 & 16 July 2007.

52. *Guardian* [UK], 16 August 2007.

53. vheadline.com, 7 September 2005.

54. *Houston Chronicle*, 27 August 2007.

55. Gerald Horne, *Cold War in a Hot Zone: The U.S. Confronts Labor and Independence Struggles in the British West Indies*, Philadelphia: Temple University Press, 2007.

56. *Los Angeles Times*, 9 April 2006.

57. *New York Times*, 23 August 2007.

58. *Indian Country Today*, 27 June 2007.

59. *Washington Times*, 14 July 2006.

60. *Financial Times*, 23 March 2007.

61. *Houston Chronicle*, 18 September 2007.

62. *Financial Times*, 25 August 2006.

63. *Los Angeles Times*, 24 June 2006.

64. BlackAmericaWeb.com, 25 July 2007.

65. *Xinhua* [China], 19 September 2007.

66. *Sydney Morning Herald*, 18 September 2007.

67. *New York Times*, 6 June 2001.

68. *Columbia Journalism Review*, 6 May 2007.

69. *Los Angeles Times*, 5 May 2007.

70. *Financial Times*, 7 June 2007.

71. *New York Times*, 16 August 2007.

72. *Washington Post*, 27 December 2001.

73. *Wall Street Journal*, 28-29 July 2007.

74. *People's Weekly World*, 28 April-4 May 2007.

75. *New York Times*, 13 July 2007.

76. *London Observer*, 22 July 2001.

5: EUROPE BITES BACK

1. *Financial Times*, 20 April 2007.

2. *New York Times*, 13 June 2001.

3. *Financial Times*, 3 April 2007,

4. *New York Times*, 26 January 2001.

5. *Wall Street Journal*, 17 September 2007.

6. *Financial Times*, 20 September 2007.

7. *Ibid.*, 22 March 2007.

8. *Financial Times*, 18 July 2007.

9. *Ibid.*, 9 June 2007.
10. *New York Times*, 7 March 2000.
11. *Ibid.*, 20 September 2002.
12. *Financial Times*, 20 April 2007.
13. *New York Times*, 17 February 2007.
14. *Washington Post*, 4 November 2005.
15. afterdowningstreet.org, 3 May 2007.
16. *Washington Post*, 11 May 2001.
17. *Ibid.*, 24 July 2000.
18. *Financial Times*, 26 January 2007.
19. *Asia Times*, 3 May 2006.
20. *The Observer* [UK], 16 February 2003.
21. *Washington Post*, 4 August 2000.
22. *Washington Post*, 9 January 2000.
23. *Ibid.*, 10 April 2001.
24. *Ibid.*, 4 October 2000.
25. *Washington Post,* 10 February 2000.
26. *South China Morning Post*, 21 July 2000.
27. *Washington Post*, 19 November 2000.
28. *Ibid.*, 13 January 2001.
29. *Washington Post*, 15 August 2005.
30. *China Daily*, 27 March 2007.
31. *Los Angeles Times*, 18 March 2006.
32. *Asia Times*, 24 March 2006.
33. *Financial Times*, 11 June 2007.
34. *Ibid.*, 26 July 2007.
35. *New York Times*, 4 April 2007.
36. *Lebanese Daily Star*, 2 November 2006.
37. *Teheran Times*, 21 December 2006.
38. *South China Morning Post*, 7 February 2001.
39. *Financial Times*, 6 June 2007.
40. *Financial Times*, 19 April 2007.
41. *Washington Times*, 6 May 2000.
42. *Financial Times*, 30 March 2007.
43. *Los Angeles Times*, 2 July 2007.
44. *New York Times*, 16 August 2007.
45. *Asia Times*, 14 August 2007.
46. *South China Morning Post*, 7 June 2000.
47. h-net.org/diplo, 20 April 2001.
48. portside.org, 28 March 2001.
49. *New York Times*, 12 June 2001.
50. *Ibid.*, 22 July 2001.
51. *Financial Times*, 24 September 2007.

6: AFRICA ARISES

1. *New Africa* [UK], July 2006.

2. irinnews.org [United Nations], 23 March 2006.

3. *Financial Times*, 18 May 2007.

4. *Ibid.*, 27 October 2006.

5. *Mail & Guardian* [South Africa], 18 September 2007.

6. *Ibid.*, 3 October 2007.

7. *San Jose Mercury News*, 20 February 2000.

8. blackelectorate.com, 11 April 2001.

9. guerrillanews.com, 18 June 2001.

10. Unfortunately, despite the frequency that Zimbabwe appears in the U.S. news media, few are aware of the history of Washington's engagement there. See e.g. Gerald Horne, *From the Barrel of a Gun: The U.S. and the War Against Zimbabwe, 1965-1980*, Chapel Hill: University of North Carolina Press, 2001.

11. *Zimbabwe Herald*, 23 April 2007.

12. *New African*, August/September 2006.

13. *Financial Times*, 28 June 2006.

14. *USA Today*, 1 May 2006.

15. irinnews.org, 17 April 2006.

16. irinnews.org, 14 December 2001.

17. *New York Times*, 19 September 2002.

18. *Asia Times*, 11 March 2003.

19. *Financial Times*, 1 March 2006.

20. irinnews, 30 September 2005.

21. stephenlewisfoundation.org, 12 June 2007.

22. Gerald Horne, *The Deepest South: The U.S., Brazil and the African Slave Trade*, New York: New York University Press, 2007.

23. *New African*, July 2006.

24. *Washington Post*, 26 July 2005.

25. africaaction.org/resources/ejournal.php, 7 March 2003.

26. *Asia Times*, 3 October 2006.

27. blackcommentator, 19 July 2007.

28. *Final Call*, 10 July 2007.

29. *This Day* [Nigeria], 14 September 2007.

30. *New York Amsterdam News*, 13-19 September 2007.

31. irinnews, 18 April 2000.

32. *Guardian* [UK], 28 April 2007.

33. *New York Times*, 16 May 2007.

34. *Los Angeles Times*, 14 May 2006.

35. *London Review of Books*, 8 March 2007.

36. *Guardian*, 16 May 2007.

37. *Los Angeles Times*, 11 June 2007.

38. fpif.org [Foreign Policy in Focus], 20 June 2007.

39. globalresearch.ca, 20 May 2007.

40. *Business Week*, 14 August 2007.

41. africapolicy.org, 16 September 2001.

42. africapolicy.org, 12 April 2001.

43. *Chicago Sun-Times*, 20 February 2007.

44. allafrica.com, 30 August 2007.

45. *Los Angeles Times*, 9 April 2007.
46. corporatepredators.org, 1 August 2000.
47. *Boston Globe*, 7 June 2001.
48. hrw.org, 7 November 2001.
49. *Washington Post*, 18 October 2000.
50. irinnews.org, 30 May 2007.
51. *The New Republic*, 17 April 2000.
52. *The Sowetan* [South Africa], 12 July 2000.
53. *Los Angeles Times*, 24 August 2007.
54. stratfor.com, 7 June 2002.
55. africafocus.org, 17 July 2006.
56. *Washington Post*, 26 January 2001.
57. *Japan Times*, 12 August 2007.
58. *Jamaica Observer*, 19 March 2005.
59. *Press Association Newsfile*, 23 March 2007.
60. *New York Amsterdam News*, 25-31 January 2007.

7: U.S. IMPERIALISM UNBOUND?

1. *New York Times*, 21 August 2007.
2. *Business Week*, 12 March 2007.
3. *Los Angeles Times*, 20 April 2006.
4. *Asia Times*, 23 March 2006.
5. *South China Morning Post*, 15 January 2001.
6. *Financial Times*, 14 July 2006.
7. *Financial Times*, 16 February 2007.
8. *Asia Times*, 3 April 2006.
9. *Los Angeles Times*, 4 August 2007.
10. *New York Times*, 21 April 2007.
11. *Toronto Star*, 14 January 2001.
12. *Financial Times*, 3 April 2007.
13. *Financial Times*, 26 January 2007.
14. *Washington Post*, 17 May 2005.
15. *Business Week*, 14 August 2007.
16. *Asia Times*, 14 August 2002.
17. *Los Angeles Times*, 10 March 2002.
18. *Los Angeles Times*, 30 June 2006.
19. *San Francisco Chronicle*, 30 May 2007.
20. *New York Times*, 9 June 2007.
21. *Guardian*, 26 April 2006.
22. *Financial Times*, 9-10 June 2007.
23. *Washington Times*, 29 June 2006.
24. *Los Angeles Times*, 31 January 2007.
25. *Financial Times*, 31 May 2007.
26. *Los Angeles Times*, 31 May 2007.
27. *Los Angeles Times*, 31 January 2007.
28. *Financial Times*, 26 January 2007.

29. *Guardian*, 27 May 2005.

30. *Los Angeles Times*, 14 August 2007.

31. *New York Times*, 7 June 2007.

32. *Guardian*, 23 February 2007.

33. *Financial Times*, 6 June 2007.

34. *New York Times*, 6 June 2007.

35. *Los Angeles Times*, 24 September 2007.

36. *Washington Post*, 19 September 2002.

37. *Washington Post*, 30 May 2003.

38. *Washington Post*, 12 November 2005.

349. *Financial Times*, 7 September 2006.

40. *Guardian*, 29 September 2007.

41. *Washington Post*, 28 March 2001.

42. *New York Times*, 26 May 2007.

43. *Financial Times*, 14 May 2007.

44. *Financial Times*, 3-4 February 2007.

45. *Financial Times*, 7-8 April 2007.

46. *New York Times*, 12 March 2007.

47. *The Independent* [UK], 26 March 2006.

48. *Guardian*, 28 April 2007.

49. *Granma* [Cuba], 20 May 2007.

50. C. Ford Runge and Benjamin Senauer, "How Biofuels Could Starve the Poor," *Foreign Affairs*, 86(Number 3, May-June 2007): 41-53.

51. *Observer* [UK], 23 April 2000.

52. *Inter Press Service*, 28 June 2007.

53. *Washington Post*, 4 August 2000.

54. *New York Newsday*, 17 November 2005.

55. *Xinhua* [China], 2 July 2005.

8: FUTURE WARS? FIGHTING BACK!

1. *New York Times*, 7 May 2001.

2. *The Nation*, 29 January 2001; spacecom.af.mil. /usspace, 28 April 2001; *Florida Today*, 9 February 2001.

3. *Washington Post*, 29 March 2005.

4. *Reuters*, 3 October 2007.

5. *Washington Times*, 30 March 2007.

6. *New York Times*, 24 May 2007.

7. *Washington Post,* 18 October 2006.

8. *China Daily*, 28 February 2005.

9. tomdispatch.com, 2 April 2005.

10. *New York Times*, 25 January 2007.

11. foreignpolicy-infocus.org,/republicanrule.commentary_body.html, 31 January 2001.

12. *Le Monde Diplomatique*, August 2007.

13. globalresearch.ca, 27 September 2004.

14. Gerald Horne, "Race Backwards: Genes, Violence and Genocide,"

Covert Action Quarterly, 1(Number 43, Winter 1992-1993): 29-35.

15. *Houston Chronicle*, 3 October 2007.

16. *Los Angeles Times*, 6 September 2007.

17. madre.org/articles, 6 May 2007.

18. *Washington Post*, 31 May 2000.

19. *Associated Press*, 24 June 2007.

20. *Los Angeles Times*, 5 April 2005.

21. Aimee Allison and David Solnit, *Army of None: Strategies to Counter Military Recruitment, End War and Build a Better World*, New York: Seven Stories Press, 2007.

22. *Seattle Times*, 25 June 2005.

23. *Final Call*, 5 June 2007.

24. *Miami Herald*, 8 September 2005.

25. *People's Weekly World*, 8 September 2005.

26. *Village Voice*, 19-25 February 2003.

27. uswa.org/uswa/program/content/index.php, 31 July 2007.

28. *Boston Globe*, 1 March 2003.

29. icftu.org, 22 January 2001.

30. ilr.cornell.edu/globallaborinstitute/events/climatechangeconference, 15 May 2007.

31. *Los Angeles Times*, 15 May 2000.

32. *USA Today*, 22 August 2001.

33. irinnews.org, 28 January 2000.

34. *Asia Times*, 4 April 2007.

35. *The Globalist*, 3 June 2005.

36. *Indian Country Today*, 26 September 2007.

37. *Indian Country Today*, 27 June 2007.

38. *Indian Country Today*, 30 May 2007.

39. See e.g. Gerald Horne, *Communist Front? The Civil Rights Congress, 1946-1956*, London: Associated University Presses, 1988.

40. *Indian Country Today*, 25 April 2007.

41. Gerald Horne, *The White Pacific: U.S. Imperialism and Black Slavery in the South Seas after the Civil War*, Honolulu: University of Hawaii Press, 2007.

42. *New York Times*, 11 May 2000.

43. *Associated Press*, 10 May 2000.

44. *New York Times*, 1 May 2007.

A

Abdullah II, King, 26, 42
Abramoff, Jack 34
Abu Ghraib, 18, 107, 123
ACLU, 122
Accenture, 61
Afghanistan, 4, 5, 7, 20, 21ff., 84, 85, 94-5
AFL-CIO, 17, 80, 136; see also, U.S. labor
Africa, and arms, 99; bases in, 105; and China, 98ff., 103; and famine, 112; and labor solidarity, 139; loans to, 109-10; oil resources of, 101, 104, 106, 108-09; and Pentagon training, 105-08; see also separate African countries
African Development Bank, 99
African Union, 107, 109, 113
AFRICOM, 106-07
ALBA, 80
Algeria, 106
Al Qaeda 25,27, 29, 30, 44, 90, 121
Al-Rajhi, Sulaiman, 24
All-China Federation of Trade Unions, 66
Alliant Techsystems, 34
Amicus, 18
ANC, 7
Angola, 101-02
anti-Sovietism, 4, 7, 15, 84
Arbusto Energy, 32
Asia Satellite Telecommunications, 65
Asian Development Bank, 58
Atomic Energy Agency, 47
Atta, Mohammed, 24
Australia, 55

B

Baker, James A.,III, 32, 49
Balkan countries, 38, 95-6
Bhutto, Benazir, 24
Bin Laden, Osama, 4, 20, 23, 24, 33, 44, 71, 105, 109
Blackwater, 34-5
Blair, Tony, 45
Blix, Hans, 37
Boeing, 6, 32, 54, 61, 86, 87, 88, 122, 129, 132
Bosnia, 23
Brazil, 79

Breakefield, Xandra 12
Bremer, L. Paul "Jerry," 36
Brzezinski, Zbigniew 5
Buchanan, Pat 73
Bush, George H.W., 13, 33, 35, 41, 116
Bush, George W., and climate change, 126-8; and corruption, 5, 6,33; lawlessness of, 120-23; amd medical lobby, 30, 32, 68-9; and military buildup, 6; and N. Korea, 60; and oil, 32, 50, 58; and veterans' needs, 40-41
Bush, William "Uncle Bucky," 5, 6, 32

C

CAFTA, 76, 80
Cameroon, 102-03
Canada, and trade, 72-3
CARICOM, 112, 113
Carlyle (Group), 32-3
Carter, Jimmy, and Afghanistan, 5; and Israel, 41
Castro, Fidel, 67, 72, 127
Cerberus Capital, 54
Chad, 102, l05, l08
Chavez, Hugo, 53, 75, 77, 79, 118
Chemical Weapons Convention, 132
Cheney, Dick 6,34, 44, 106, 135
Chevron 76, 77, 78, 109
Chin, Vincent, 58
China,and Africa, 98-104; and Cuba, 12, 67; economic growth of, 7, 13, 52-4, 87; and India, 60-61; and Iran, 53, and Israel, 13, 45; and Japan, 57-8; and labor's rights, 66, 139; and N.Korea, 53; and outer space policy, 130-33; and Russia, 14-15, 88-90; and S. Korea, 60; trade w/U.S., 12, 14, 120-21; and Vietnam, 60. *see also* United States and China
Chiquita Brands, 75, 80, 86
Chirac, Jacques, 10-11
Chrysler, 8, 53, 54, 58, 115
CIA, 90, 97; and E.Africa, 105, 109; and Jordan, 43; and Laos,60; and overseas prisons, 122-23; recruiting, 134; and SAVAK, 43; and Taliban, 20-22
Cisco Systems, 61
Citicorp 25, 61